APP for Reading and Writing

Year 4

Christine Moorcroft

Contents

Pearson Education Limited, a company incorporated in England and Wales, having its registered office at Edinburgh Gate, Harlow, Essex, CM20 2JE. Registered company number: 872828

www.pearsonschools.co.uk

Text © Pearson Education Limited 2010

First published 2010

14 13 12 11 10

10 9 8 7 6 5 4 3 2 1

British Library Cataloguing in Publication Data

A catalogue record for this book is available from the British Library.

ISBN 978 0 435 04153 3

Literacy consultant: Anne Derry

Typeset by Zed

Illustrated by Mike Lacey **20, 21, 22, 24, 51, 52, 53, 54**; Robin Lawrie **9, 10, 11, 14, 64, 65, 67**; Matt Ward **30, 31, 34, 40, 41, 42, 43**.

Cover illustration by Clive Goodyer © Pearson Education Limited

Printed and bound in the UK by Henry Ling Ltd

Introduction

APP for Reading and Writing has been developed to help you to assess accurately your pupils' progress and attainment in reading and writing skills, using texts and questions designed to elicit evidence for specific assessment points. This Year 4 book contains six tasks, covering the Assessment Foci for National Curriculum Levels 3 and 4.

How to use this book

The tasks in this book are designed to support the periodic assessment that is a key part of the 'Assessing Pupils' Progress' (APP) evidence gathering. The tasks help you to gather evidence to support your own professional understanding of each child's level of achievement. The tasks should help you form a good understanding of the National Curriculum level at which children are working. They have been written to work in conjunction with, and should be used alongside, the QCDA and National Strategy APP Assessment Guidance charts and the Standards files. Copies of the Assessment Guidance charts are included on pages 6 and 7.

Gathering assessment evidence to address Assessment Foci

The Assessment Guidance charts on pages 6 and 7 outline the Assessment Foci for Reading and Writing, all of which are covered by the tasks in this book. The chart on the top of page 5 gives an overview of this coverage. Where a child is not demonstrating the reading and / or writing evidence expected at Level 3 in these tasks, you may want to find an equivalent task from the Year 3 book to collect evidence across Levels 2 and 3. The tasks cover the same Assessment Foci although the genre of the stimulus pieces may differ.

Using the tasks in the classroom

There are six tasks in this book, which can be integrated into your school's literacy planning. The tasks are based on stimulus pieces from a variety of fiction and non-fiction text types. Each of the tasks allows you to collect evidence for both reading and writing. The tasks may also provide evidence about pupils' attainment and progress in speaking and listening. We recommend that children carry out the reading activity first, so that they are familiar with the stimulus piece before completing the writing activity. Each task is designed to take approximately 30 minutes to complete. The tasks will support your evidence gathering, but will not be the sole basis for your judgements about pupils' achievement.

Teacher Sheets

Each task has a Teacher Sheet offering an overview of the task, the key concepts it targets and the related Renewed Framework unit and objectives it covers.

Reading tasks

You can choose between working with a small group for guided reading, or asking children to read and answer the questions independently. The guided reading questions are supplied on the Teacher Sheet for each task. You might like to use these to collect evidence through open discussion, in which case you can use the Reading Responses Levelling Guidance sheet to capture notes about individual oral responses. If you would rather ask children to work independently, the questions and space to answer them are provided on the photocopiable sheets for each task. The bold questions on the Teacher Sheet are those that are included on the photocopiable Reading Response Sheets.

For both guided and independent reading, the questions focus on two or three AFs, and the assessment guidance sheet gives you examples of the kind of responses children may give, and the level this would indicate.

Writing tasks

For writing, children complete a series of short-answer questions and a longer writing activity. Real examples of children's work are provided, along with notes to help you assess children's work for the chosen Assessment Foci. It should be noted that responses can vary within a level depending on the type of writing pupils are asked to do (e.g. some may not do as well with narrative as they do with a report). Therefore, attainment and progress for any pupil should not be expected to be totally linear.

Making assessment judgements

No single task can determine that a child is low, secure or high Level 3 or Level 4. However, observing a child working on several tasks over a period of time will provide evidence of their functioning at a particular level for reading and writing and should also give an indication of their security within that level. You will need to combine the evidence that these tasks give you with your day-to-day knowledge of a child's performance to decide how consistently the evidence fits the criteria in the Assessment Focus in order to determine whether the child's performance at that level is 'low', 'secure' or 'high'. You should also gather evidence for reading and writing from other subject areas.

A child may prove to be at different levels for different Assessment Foci, and be at a different level for reading than for writing. When you highlight the areas at which they are working on the assessment grids, you may see a 'spiky profile'; you can use this to inform your future planning to fill in any gaps in children's knowledge or skills by referring to the learning objectives that underpin that particular Assessment Focus.

Consistency and moderation

The example answers provided in this book are designed to help you gauge the level at which the children in your class are performing. However, these examples are provided as a guide only and professional judgement must be used when reviewing the evidence and making consistent judgements about children's attainment. The examples cannot cover all the different ways in which different children may respond. When you are reviewing the evidence from these tasks, along with other evidence, to make a level judgement, it is good practice to confer with a colleague who knows the children's performance in literacy to corroborate your judgement.

What to do next

At the end of each task, 'next steps' guidance is given about what teachers might do next in terms of planning for teaching and learning for the relevant AFs, referenced to the appropriate learning objectives. This guidance also points to other assessments within the book that cover those AFs.

© **Pearson Education Ltd 2010.** APP for Reading and Writing: Year 4

Assessment Foci covered by the Year 4 tasks

● = Main AFs   O = Other AFs

READING							
	AF1	AF2	AF3	AF4	AF5	AF6	AF7
Task 1: The Evacuee	O	●	●		●		O
Task 2: I Asked the Little Boy	O	●	●	O	●	O	
Task 3: How Does It Work?	O	O	O	●	●	●	
Task 4: The Thief in Ash Road School	O	O	●		●	●	
Task 5: The Second Legion	O	O	O	●	●		●
Task 6: Improving the Neighbourhood	O	●		O	●	●	

WRITING								
	AF1	AF2	AF3	AF4	AF5	AF6	AF7	AF8
Task 1: The Evacuee	●		●	O	O	●		O
Task 2: I Asked the Little Boy	●				O		●	O
Task 3: How Does It Work?		●	O		●	●		O
Task 4: The Thief in Ash Road School	●		●	●	O		O	O
Task 5: The Second Legion	O	●				●	●	O
Task 6: Improving the Neighbourhood	O	●	●	O			●	

Renewed Framework for Literacy Reading and Writing Objectives covered by the Year 4 tasks

7. **Understanding and interpreting texts**
    7.1   Identify and summarise evidence from a text to support a hypothesis
    7.2   Deduce characters' reasons for behaviour from their actions and explain how ideas are developed in non-fiction texts
    7.3   Use knowledge of different organisational features of texts to find information effectively
    7.4   Use knowledge of word structures and origins to develop their understanding of word meanings
    7.5   Explain how writers use figurative and expressive language to create images and atmosphere
8. **Engaging with and responding to texts**
    8.2   Interrogate texts to deepen and clarify understanding and response
9. **Creating and shaping texts**
    9.1   Develop and refine ideas in writing using planning and problem-solving strategies
    9.2   Use settings and characterisation to engage readers' interest
    9.3   Summarise and shape material and ideas from different sources to write convincing and informative non-narrative texts
    9.5   Choose and combine words, images and other features for particular effects
10. **Text structure and organisation**
    10.1 Organise text into paragraphs to distinguish between different information, events or processes
    10.2 Use adverbs and conjunctions to establish cohesion within paragraphs
11. **Sentence structure and punctuation**
    11.1 Clarify meaning and point of view by using varied sentence structure (phrases, clauses and adverbials)
    11.2 Use commas to mark clauses, and use the apostrophe for possession

Task	Renewed Framework objectives covered
Task 1: The Evacuee	7.2, 7.5, 8.2, 9.2, 10.1, 11.2
Task 2: I Asked the Little Boy	7.1, 7.5, 8.2, 9.1, 9.3, 9.5
Task 3: How Does It Work?	7.2, 7.4, 9.1, 10.1, 10.2
Task 4: The Thief in Ash Road School	7.1, 7.2, 8.2, 9.1, 11.1
Task 5: The Second Legion	7. 1, 7.2, 7.3, 7.4, 9.2, 9.5
Task 6: Improving the Neighbourhood	7.1, 7.2, 7.5, 9.3, 9.5, 10.1

QCDA Reading Assessment Guidelines: Levels 3 and 4

	AF1 – use a range of strategies, including accurate decoding of text, to read for meaning	AF2 – understand, describe, select or retrieve information, events or ideas from texts and use quotation and reference to text	AF3 – deduce, infer or interpret information, events or ideas from texts	AF4 – identify and comment on the structure and organisation of texts, including grammatical and presentational features at text level	AF5 – explain and comment on writers' use of language, including grammatical and literary features at word and sentence level	AF6 – identify and comment on writers' purposes and viewpoints, and the overall effect of the text on the reader	AF7 – relate texts to their social, cultural and historical traditions
L4		**Across a range of reading:** • some relevant points identified • comments supported by some generally relevant textual reference or quotation, e.g. reference is made to appropriate section of text but is unselective and lacks focus	**Across a range of reading:** • comments make inferences based on evidence from different points in the text, e.g. interpreting a character's motive from their actions at different points • inferences often correct, but comments are not always rooted securely in the text or repeat narrative or content	**Across a range of reading:** • some structural choices identified with simple comment, e.g. 'he describes the accident first and then goes back to tell you why the child was in the road' • some basic features of organisation at text level identified, e.g. 'the writer uses bullet points for the main reasons'	**Across a range of reading:** • some basic features of writer's use of language identified, e.g. 'all the questions make you want to find out what happens next' • simple comments on writer's choices, e.g. '"disgraceful" is a good word to use to show he is upset'	**Across a range of reading:** • main purpose identified, e.g. 'it's all about why going to the dentist is important and how you should look after your teeth' • simple comments show some awareness of writer's viewpoint, e.g. 'he only tells you good things about the farm and makes the shop sound boring' • simple comment on overall effect on reader, e.g. 'the way she describes him as "ratlike" and "shifty" makes you think he's disgusting'	**Across a range of reading:** • features common to different texts or versions of the same text identified, with simple comment, e.g. characters, settings, presentational features • simple comment on the effect that the reader's or writer's context has on the meaning of texts, e.g. historical context, place, social relationships
L3	**In most reading:** • range of strategies used mostly effectively to read with fluency, understanding and expression	**In most reading:** • simple, most obvious points identified though there may also be some misunderstanding, e.g. about information from different places in the text • some comments include quotations from or references to text, but not always relevant, e.g. often retelling or paraphrasing sections of the text rather than using it to support comment	**In most reading:** • straightforward inference based on a single point of reference in the text, e.g. 'he was upset because it says "he was crying"' • responses to text show meaning established at a literal level e.g. '"walking good" means "walking carefully"' or based on personal speculation e.g. a response based on what they personally would be feeling rather than feelings of character in the text	**In most reading:** • a few basic features of organisation at text level identified, with little or no linked comment, e.g. 'it tells about all the different things you can do at the zoo'	**In most reading:** • a few basic features of writer's use of language identified, but with little or no comment, e.g. 'there are lots of adjectives' or 'he uses speech marks to show there are lots of people there'	**In most reading:** • comments identify main purpose, e.g. 'the writer doesn't like violence' • express personal response but with little awareness of writer's viewpoint or effect on reader, e.g. 'she was just horrible like my nan is sometimes'	**In most reading:** • some simple connections between texts identified, e.g. similarities in plot, topic, or books by same author, about same characters • recognition of some features of the context of texts, e.g. historical setting, social or cultural background
BL							
IE							

Overall assessment (tick one box only) Low 3 ☐ Secure 3 ☐ High 3 ☐ Low 4 ☐ Secure 4 ☐ High 4 ☐   BL = 'Below Level'   IE = 'Insufficient Evidence'

QCDA Writing Assessment Guidelines: Levels 3 and 4

	AF5 – vary sentences for clarity, purpose and effect	AF6 – write with technical accuracy of syntax and punctuation in phrases, clauses and sentences	AF3 – organise and present whole texts effectively, sequencing and structuring information, ideas and events	AF4 – construct paragraphs and use cohesion within and between paragraphs	AF1 – write imaginative, interesting and thoughtful texts	AF2 – produce texts which are appropriate to task, reader and purpose	AF7 – select appropriate and effective vocabulary	AF8 – use correct spelling	Handwriting and presentation
L4	**Across a range of writing:** • some variety in length, structure or subject of sentences • use of some subordinating connectives, e.g. if, when, because throughout the text • some variation, generally accurate, in tense and verb forms	**Across a range of writing:** • sentences demarcated accurately throughout the text, including question marks • speech marks to denote speech generally accurate, with some other speech punctuation • commas used in lists and occasionally to mark clauses, although not always accurately	**Across a range of writing:** • ideas organised by clustering related points or by time sequence • ideas are organised simply with a fitting opening and closing, sometimes linked • ideas or material generally in logical sequence but overall direction of writing not always clearly signalled	**Across a range of writing:** • paragraphs/sections help to organise content, e.g. main idea usually supported or elaborated by following sentences • within paragraphs/ sections, limited range of connections between sentences, e.g. over-use of 'also' or pronouns • some attempts to establish simple links between paragraphs/ sections not always maintained, e.g. firstly, next	**Across a range of writing:** • relevant ideas and content chosen • some ideas and material developed in detail, e.g. descriptions elaborated by adverbial and expanded noun phrases • straightforward viewpoint generally established and maintained, e.g. writing in role or maintaining a consistent stance	**Across a range of writing:** • main purpose of writing clear but not always consistently maintained • main features of selected form are clear and appropriate to purpose • style generally appropriate to task, though awareness of reader not always sustained	**Across a range of writing:** • some evidence of deliberate vocabulary choices • some expansion of general vocabulary to match topic	**Across a range of writing:** • correct spelling of – most common grammatical function words, including adverbs with -ly formation – regularly formed content/lexical words, including those with multiple morphemes – most past and present tense inflections, plurals • likely errors – homophones of some common grammatical function words – occasional phonetically plausible spelling in content/lexical words	
L3	**In most writing:** • reliance mainly on simply structured sentences, variation with support, e.g. some complex sentences • and, but, so are the most common connectives, subordination occasionally • some limited variation in use of tense and verb forms, not always secure	**In most writing:** • straightforward sentences usually demarcated accurately with full stops, capital letters, question and exclamation marks • some, limited, use of speech punctuation • comma splicing evident, particularly in narrative	**In most writing:** • some attempt to organise ideas with related points placed next to each other • openings and closings usually signalled • some attempt to sequence ideas or material logically	**In most writing:** • some internal structure within sections of text e.g. one-sentence paragraphs or ideas loosely organised • within paragraphs/ sections, some links between sentences, e.g. use of pronouns or of adverbials • movement between paragraphs/sections sometimes abrupt or disjointed	**In most writing:** • some appropriate ideas and content included • some attempt to elaborate on basic information or events, e.g. nouns expanded by simple adjectives • attempt to adopt viewpoint, though often not maintained or inconsistent, e.g. attitude expressed, but with little elaboration	**In most writing:** • purpose established at a general level • main features of selected form sometimes signalled to the reader • some attempts at appropriate style, with attention to reader	**In most writing:** • simple, generally appropriate vocabulary used, limited in range • some words selected for effect or occasion	**In most writing:** • correct spelling of – some common grammatical function words – common content/lexical words with more than one morpheme, including compound words • likely errors – some inflected endings, e.g. past tense, comparatives, adverbs – some phonetically plausible attempts at content/lexical words	**In most writing:** • legible style, shows accurate and consistent letter formation, sometimes joined
BL									
IE									

Overall assessment (tick one box only) Low 3 ☐   Secure 3 ☐   High 3 ☐   Low 4 ☐   Secure 4 ☐   High 4 ☐   BL = 'Below Level'   IE = 'Insufficient Evidence'

Task 1 The Evacuee

Aims of this task
This task is designed to help you to make judgements about children's attainment in Reading **AF2**, **AF3** and **AF5** (with opportunities to assess AF1 and AF7 as well) and Writing **AF1**, **AF3** and **AF6** (with opportunities to assess AF4, AF5 and AF8 as well). The children read and respond to an extract set in the Second World War from *Tom's Private War* by Robert Leeson. The extract is about relationships between evacuees from Liverpool and local country children. The children plan and write a story in the first person that uses dialogue.

Related Renewed Framework unit
Narrative Unit 1: Stories with historical settings

Renewed Framework objectives
7.2, 7.5, 8.2, 9.2, 10.1, 11.2

Key concepts
Reading
- retrieve information from the story referring to the text to support their answers (AF2)
- deduce how the characters in the story feel (AF3)
- identify and comment on the writer's use of dialect words (AF5)
- use the text to find out about evacuation in the Second World War (AF7)

Writing
- write imaginative and appropriate text (AF1)
- plan a story in paragraphs, making notes about the main events in each paragraph (AF3)
- write dialogue and compose well-structured and appropriately punctuated sentences (AF6)

Questions for guided reading

Starting off
Ask what the children know about evacuation in the Second World War. Why were children sent away from their parents? What sort of places were they sent to? Ask them to read the extract from the story (AF1), thinking about the feelings of the evacuees and the local children.

Read and respond
Answer the following questions as part of a group discussion:
- **How did the Liverpool children feel about the evacuation? (AF3)**
- **How did William and Molly feel about the Liverpool lad? (AF3)**
- **Why did Widow Robertson take in an evacuee? (AF2)**
- **How did William annoy the evacuee? (AF2)**
- **What are 'vaccies'? Explain how you know. (AF5)**
- **List some other words and phrases that are not Standard English. Explain what they mean. (AF5)**

Going deeper
- **What kind of character is the Liverpool lad? How can you tell? (AF3)**
- How did William, Tom and the Liverpool lad get on with one another? (AF3)
- **What does this extract tell us about evacuation during the Second World War? (AF7)**

Reflect
The author says that 'William was not going to forget'. What do you think he will do? (AF3)

Task 1 The Evacuee by Robert Leeson

It is 1939 and the Second World War has started. Tom and his gang have to cope with gas masks and blackouts. Then the evacuees arrive.

That weekend the 'vaccies' arrived from Liverpool. A coachload of them, pale and miserable, clutching cardboard suitcases, name labels tied to their coats.

Tom's mum was sorry for them. She wanted to take in a boy or girl, but the house was too crowded. Widow Robertson, though, was on her own. She took an evacuee and the whole street knew about it.

"It's a crying shame. Those snobs up Birch Lane looked the poor jiggers up and down and picked out the cleanest ones. When it was all done, this poor little chap was left."

Poor little chap? He was the same age as Tom, but hard as nails, Tom could see that, with a face like a ferret, a sharp nose and red eyes. He came out into the street just as the gang met up. William, who seemed to be in a good mood again, winked and raised his voice.

"Yeah, you know where Liverpool is – that little place across the Mersey from New Brighton."

Task 1 The Evacuee

The evacuee rose to the bait.

"It's on the map, any road, not like this dump. There's nothing here, no flicks, two shops, a load of fields and a bunch of useless cows."

"Our cows aren't useless," said William loftily.

"What use are they?"

"They give good milk, that's what."

The Liverpool lad stared in disbelief.

"Don't be gormless. You don't get milk from those mucky things. It comes clean in bottles, round our way."

The gang burst into laughter, punching each other. Even Molly, who felt sorry for him, had to grin.

The pale face reddened. He picked on Tom, who was his own size. "What are you laughing at?"

Tom choked, and said hastily, "Nowt, mate."

"It had better be nowt, kidder." The evacuee's tone was menacing. He turned on his heels and went into Widow Robertson's entry.

William looked scornfully at Tom. "Fancy letting a Scouser talk to you like that. You should've poked him one."

"Oh, forget it," said Molly hastily. But William was not going to forget.

An extract from *Tom's Private War* by Robert Leeson

Task 1 The Evacuee

1. How did the Liverpool children feel about the evacuation?

....

....

....

....

2. How did William and Molly feel about the Liverpool lad?

....

....

....

3. Why did Widow Robertson take in an evacuee?

....

....

....

4. How did William annoy the evacuee?

....

....

....

Task 1 The Evacuee

5. What are 'vaccies'? Explain how you know.

_____

_____

_____

_____

6. List some other words and phrases that are not Standard English. Explain what they mean.

_____

_____

_____

_____

_____

7. What kind of character is the Liverpool lad? How can you tell?

_____

_____

_____

_____

8. What does this extract tell us about evacuation during the Second World War?

_____

_____

_____

Task 1 The Evacuee

Main Assessment Focus: AF2 (understand, describe, select or retrieve information, events or ideas from texts and use quotation and reference to text))

Question	Exemplified responses	Grid reference	Notes
Why did Widow Robertson take in an evacuee?	Comments refer to text: 'She was on her own.'	Level 3 / bullet 2	
	Comments supported by text reference: 'She had room in her house as she lived on her own.'	Level 4 / bullet 2	
How did William annoy the evacuee?	Simple points identified: 'He called him gormless.'	Level 3 / bullet 1	
	Relevant points identified: 'He made fun of Liverpool by calling it a little place.'	Level 4 / bullet 1	

Main Assessment Focus: AF3 (deduce, infer or interpret information, events or ideas from texts)

Question	Exemplified responses	Grid reference	Notes
How did the Liverpool children feel about the evacuation?	Straightforward inference: 'Sad. It says they were "miserable"'; Might comment: 'Sad because they were going away from home.' 'Not well. It says "They were pale".' Other similar misunderstandings.	Level 2 / bullet 1	
	Inferences made from different points in text: 'Miserable, because they had to go away from home and they had to live with people they didn't know.'	Level 4 / bullet 1	
What kind of character is the Liverpool lad? How can you tell?	Understands meaning: 'He must be nervous' (personal response); 'He's nasty' (from 'sharp eyes and 'face like a ferret'); 'He's angry' (from 'face reddened').	Level 3 / bullet 2	
	Inferences correct: 'He was small but tough because it says he's "little" and "hard as nails".' Comments on 'ferret' description – mean / sly.	Level 4 / bullet 2	

Main Assessment Focus: AF5 (explain and comment on writers' use of language, including grammatical and literary features at word and sentence level)

Question	Exemplified responses	Grid reference	Notes
What are 'vaccies'? Explain how you know.	Identifies use of language: 'Evacuees. It's short for evacuees.'	Level 3 / bullet 1	
	The above, plus explanation: 'It sounds like part of the word / I've heard it before.'	Level 4 / bullet 2	
List some other words and phrases that are not Standard English. Explain what they mean.	Identifies most of the following: jiggers (perhaps as 'dancers' – misunderstood), flicks, gormless, nowt, kidder, poked him one. Explains some: gormless / stupid, nowt / nothing.	Level 3 / bullet 1	
	Identifies nearly all. Most explanations correct. Might comment that they are used in speech.	Level 4 / bullet 2	

Other Assessment Focus: AF7 (relate texts to their social, cultural and historical traditions)

Question	Exemplified responses	Grid reference	Notes
What does this passage tell us about evacuation during the Second World War?	Recognises some features: 'Evacuees came from Liverpool. They didn't know about cows.'	Level 3 / bullet 2	
	Simple comments on the historical context: 'Evacuees were sent from the cities to stay in the country.'	Level 4 / bullet 2	

Exemplified responses matched to levels of attainment are provided as a guide. As always, professional judgement must be used when assessing pupils' learning progression and a range of evidence should be gathered for each AF.

Task 1 The Evacuee

1. Imagine you are an evacuee sent to live in the country. Write what the local children might say to you.

   REMEMBER! Some are friendly to you, but others are not.

   [ ]   [ ]

   [ ]   [ ]

2. Plan the story in which you are an evacuee. Write notes about what is said or happens in each paragraph.

1.	2.	3.
4.	5.	6.

3. Write your story on a separate piece of paper.

   REMEMBER!
   - Use the rules for writing speech.
   - Use long and short sentences.
   - Use words that link the sentences together.

 © Pearson Education Ltd 2010. APP for Reading and Writing: Year 4

Task 1 The Evacuee

A pupil response within the range for Level 3 might be:

Question 1 (AF6)

- Where appropriate, might use exclamation marks or question marks. Most sentences accurately demarcated with full stops and capital letters.

Question 2 (AF3)

- Boxes completed mainly in note form, showing some grasp of the logical sequence of key events in a story.

Question 3 (AF1, AF3, AF4, AF5, AF6, AF8)

AF1

The content and ideas are appropriately related to wartime evacuation: going to the station and embarking on a train journey to the country.

There is use of simple adjectives to expand nouns: 'hot', 'cold', 'many', 'lucky', 'great'.

AF3

The opening and ending are signalled 'Today I woke…'; 'It seems like…'.

The story has a logical sequence: waking; thinking about evacuation; saying goodbye; going to the station; the journey; arriving at the destination; exploring the new temporary home.

AF4

The writer attempts to use pronouns to link sentences: 'she', 'we'.

Adverbials feature in some sentences: 'While I was having breakfast', 'that day', 'When I got there', 'On the train'.

AF5

Most sentences have a simple structure, but some are complex and include connectives: 'while', 'because', 'when' – introducing subordination. This helps with variation: long and short sentences.

There is variation in tense, with narrative mainly in the past and dialogue in the present. Tenses are not completely secure: 'Who would I be with?'; 'Where am I going to be?'; 'It seems like…'.

AF6

Sentences are mainly straightforward and all are demarcated with capital letters and full stops, question marks or exclamation marks.

Attempts speech punctuation, but not secure: a full stop where a comma should be and the final quotation mark reversed.

Grammatical errors occur: 'Me and Victoria'; 'Me, my brothers and Victoria…'.

> The Evacuee
>
> Today, I woke up hot but I was cold inside. I stamped my foot because I knew it was my evacuation day. There were so many questions buzzing in my head while I was getting dressed. Who would I be with? Where am I going to be? While I was having breakfast I said bye to my mum because she was working for the war that day. "I'll miss you." I said. I walked to the train staition with my brothers. When I got there I had to run as the train had nearly left. I felt really unlucky. On the train I met a girl called Victoria. We had loads of jokes to tell each other. The train came to a holt. Me and Victoria jumped off. Me, my brothers and Victoria were lucky. We were the first ones to be picked so we didn't have to wait. We all went to the same place. We had a great adventure exploring the house from top to bottom, seeing lots of intresting things on the way. It seems like everything is an adventure for me!

AF8

Most grammatical function words and common content / lexical words are spelled correctly: 'knew' (self-corrected), 'there', 'were', 'while', 'who', 'would'.

Compound words are spelled correctly: 'breakfast', 'everything'. The spellings of 'station', 'interesting' and 'halt' ('staition', 'intresting', 'holt') are phonetically plausible.

Task 1 The Evacuee

A pupil response within the range for Level 4 might be:

Question 1 (AF6)
- End of sentence punctuation accurate. Might use commas, if appropriate.

Question 2 (AF3)
- Main events of story recorded in note form in an order that makes sense. An opening and ending are indicated.

Question 3 (AF1, AF3, AF4, AF5, AF6, AF8)

AF1

The content and ideas are relevant, understands from the model text town children's ignorance of the countryside.

Some imaginative details are included through adverbials and expanded noun clauses: 'a lovely breakfast of fresh (they had been laid that morning) eggs', 'a pen full of white furry things that all came bounding towards me'.

The writer maintains his / her role in the first person.

AF3

The time sequence is secure and uses appropriate time connectives: 'When we got there'; 'The next morning'; 'The next thing I knew'.

The opening and closing are imaginative, setting the scene and rounding off the story / chapter.

AF4

Paragraphs are used to structure the text into sections in appropriate chronological order.

Sentences are linked by adverbials: 'The next morning', 'After that', 'The next thing I knew', but there is some repetition of 'when'.

AF5

Repetition in the use of 'I' to start sentences, but there is variety in subject and structure (with some use of the passive): 'It was', 'When', 'I was picked', 'After that Mr Jones showed...'.

Variation in sentence length and subordinating connectives are used: 'It was the first time that I...'; 'although, when we got there'.

Variation in verb forms and tenses, including use of the pluperfect tense and the passive.

AF6

The opening and ending sentences are demarcated accurately with capital letters, full stops and exclamation marks.

Speech marks are used accurately. Commas are used to demarcate clauses and, in one case, there is an attempt at parentheses.

AF8

Common grammatical function words, content / lexical words, past tense and inflected endings are spelled correctly: 'there', 'were', 'which', 'sausages', 'sandwiches', 'thanked', 'scrambled'.

I was on the train to Six Bells and, very, very excited! It was the first time that I had been to Wales and although I hated Hitler I secretly thanked him for sending me on this great trip! When we got there we had a drink than we were picked by all different families. I was picked by Mr Jones, who owned a farm on the mountain-side.

The next morning Mrs Jones made a lovely breakfast of fresh (they had been laid that morning) eggs, which were scrambled, and sausages. After that Mr Jones showed me around the farm. He showed me how to milk a cow, and also how to ride a horse! We went indoors for some sandwiches, and Mr Jones said that I could explore the farm by myself after lunch. That was just what I did!
I went to a pen full of white furry things that all came bounding towards me when I opened the gate. The next thing I knew, I was running across the mountain side, and Mr Jones was at the window, telling me to watch out for the sheep! I didn't know what he was talking about, and then it suddenly dawned on me that these were sheep! The things that were chasing me were sheep! I gave them their food and they went back to their pen. When I was back in the farmhouse I helped Mrs Jones prepare tea. When we sat down and ate it, all of us were laughing about the way the sheep chased me!
"I think I'm definetly going to like it here!" I said happily.

Task 1 The Evacuee

Reading

Next steps for developing AF2

Children will benefit from further practice in answering questions that require them to understand, describe and retrieve information, events or ideas from a story. Useful questions might be:

- When was the story set? Which words and phrases in the story are clues?
- What did x do when y...? Where does it tell us this in the story?
- What happened when x said ...?

This activity should be part of a range of evidence gathered for AF2. Evidence for AF2 can be gathered from various sources, such as:

- discussion of information texts (including electronic texts), instructions, newspaper reports, television or radio news broadcasts, television drama, serials, films;
- note-making for other subjects: e.g. geography, science, history.

All tasks in this book provide opportunities to gather evidence for AF2.

Next steps for developing AF3

Children will benefit from further practice in answering inferential questions and referencing the text to support answers. Useful questions you could ask when reading a story together might be:

- Why do you think x said ...?
- Which words in the story make you think that?
- Did x and y feel the same about ...? Which words tell you that?
- How would you feel if ...? Did x feel like that? Which words tell you that?

This activity should be part of a range of evidence gathered for AF3. Evidence for AF3 can be gathered from various sources, such as:

- observations during guided and shared reading;
- responding to pictures, films, broadcasts etc;
- writing thought bubbles for characters in a story;
- whenever children need to read between the lines in a text in another subject areas: e.g. history, RE or PSHE.

Task 2 on pages 19 to 28, Task 3 on pages 29 to 38, Task 4 on pages 39 to 49 and Task 5 on pages 50 to 61 provide other opportunities to gather evidence for AF3.

Next steps for developing AF5

Children will benefit from further practice in answering questions about language and grammatical features and identifying these in texts. Questions like those below could be asked when reading a story together:

- Which words show that x is trying to...?
- Which words show that x feels...?
- How does the writer show how the characters speak?
- Where does the writer use dialect words?
- Which verbs show different kinds of laugh / walk / other movement?

This activity should be part of a range of evidence gathered for AF5. Evidence for AF5 can be gathered from various sources, such as:

- observations during discussions of poetry;
- responding to performance poems, rhymes and jingles;
- whenever there are opportunities to think about the effects of words or devices such as repetition.

All tasks in this book provide opportunities to gather evidence for AF5.

Task 1 The Evacuee

Writing

Next steps for developing AF1

You could develop a thoughtful approach in the children and help them to create realistic historical stories through linking this to what they have learned in history. The following discussion points and activities will help:

- How children or others at the time dressed, amused themselves and so on.
- Transport and homes at the time.
- Characters' concerns or worries that were, and still are, meaningful.

This should be part of a range of writing activities from which evidence is gathered for AF1. Evidence for AF1 can also be gathered from:

- generating ideas for writing other narrative texts and poetry;
- generating ideas for writing non-fiction.

Task 2 on pages 19 to 28, Task 4 on pages 39 to 49, Task 5 on pages 50 to 61 and Task 6 on pages 62 to 71 also provide opportunities to gather evidence for AF1.

Next steps for developing AF3

You could develop the children's understanding of how to organise and present stories through discussion points and activities such as:

- How they began a chapter or paragraph: how it sets the scene for the story and introduces the main character.
- Listing the key events in a story in the correct order, using a flow-chart.
- Checking each other's stories and writing questions about it.
- How they end a chapter or story, and why. Did they 'tie up all the loose ends'?

This should be part of a range of writing activities from which evidence is gathered for AF3. Evidence for AF3 can also be gathered from:

- planning, organising and writing other genres of narrative text and playscripts;
- planning, organising and writing poetry;
- planning, organising and writing non-fiction texts.

Task 3 on pages 29 to 38, Task 4 on pages 39 to 49 and Task 6 on pages 62 to 71 provide other opportunities to gather evidence for AF3.

Next steps for developing AF6

You could develop the children's understanding of syntax, punctuation and sentence structure through the following activities, discussion and questioning:

- Reading one another's writing and looking for missing punctuation. Talk about how these help the reader to make sense of the writing.
- Adding details to sentences through extra clauses that are marked by commas.
- Checking for over-use of exclamation marks or for unnecessary commas.

This should be part of a range of writing activities from which evidence is gathered for AF6. Evidence for AF6 can also be gathered from:

- other narrative writing where punctuation is important for meaning or effect;
- writing that includes phrases and clauses linked by time or logical connectives;
- transcribing a short dialogue, using speech marks to make clear what is said and by whom.

Task 3 on pages 29 to 38 and Task 5 on pages 50 to 61 provide other opportunities to gather evidence for AF6.

Task 2 I Asked the Little Boy

Aims of this task

This task is designed to help you to make judgements about children's attainment in Reading **AF2, AF3** and **AF5** (with opportunities to assess AF1, AF4, and AF6 as well) and Writing **AF1** and **AF7** (with opportunities to assess AF5 and AF8 as well). The children read and respond to a poem that creates images of colours using similes. The children create their own colour similes and then write a similes poem.

Related Renewed Framework unit

Poetry Unit 1: Creating images

Renewed Framework objectives

7.1, 7.5, 8.2, 9.1, 9.3, 9.5

Key concepts

Reading
- describe ideas from a poem (AF2)
- interpret ideas from a poem (AF3)
- comment on the rhyme pattern and structure of a poem (AF4)
- identify and describe similes (AF5)
- discuss personal responses to a poem (AF6)

Writing
- write a similes poem using the poem as a model (AF1, AF5)
- write similes for colours and the senses (AF7)

Questions for guided reading

Starting off

Tell the children they are going to read a poem about colours and give them a 'taster' by reading 'And red is like a trumpet sound'. Ask them if they think there is anything unusual about it, e.g. how can a colour be like a sound? Ask them to read the poem (AF1) and to imagine the things the poet describes (AF6).

Read and respond

Answer the following questions and prompts as part of a group discussion:
- **In the poem, what is yellow like? (AF2)**
- **What colour must be like a thunderstorm? (AF2)**
- **Choose another simile from the poem and explain the comparison. (AF5)**
- **What makes red a good colour for a trumpet sound? (AF5)**
- **What is unusual about the coloured things in the poem? (AF3)**
- **What rhyming pattern does the poem have? (AF4)**

Going deeper
- **How does the little boy in the poem use his senses? (AF3)**
- **How does the poem make you feel? (AF6)**

Reflect

Discuss how the poem seems to speed up and then slow down. The children could re-read it aloud and identify the points where this happens. (AF4)

Task 2 I Asked the Little Boy

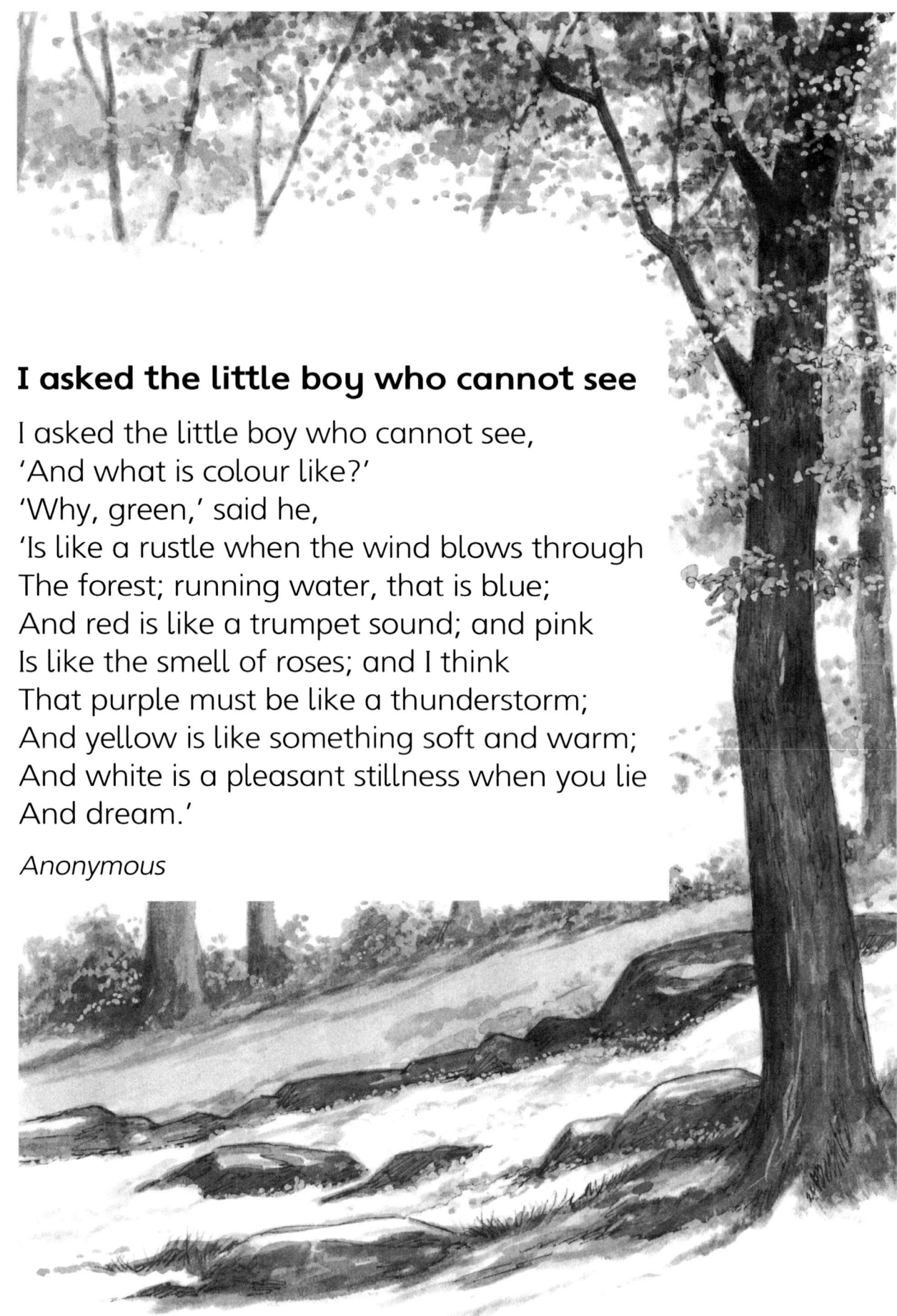

I asked the little boy who cannot see

I asked the little boy who cannot see,
'And what is colour like?'
'Why, green,' said he,
'Is like a rustle when the wind blows through
The forest; running water, that is blue;
And red is like a trumpet sound; and pink
Is like the smell of roses; and I think
That purple must be like a thunderstorm;
And yellow is like something soft and warm;
And white is a pleasant stillness when you lie
And dream.'

Anonymous

Task 2 I Asked the Little Boy

1. In the poem, what is yellow like?

2. What colour must be like a thunderstorm?

3. Choose another simile from the poem and explain the comparison.

4. What makes red a good colour for a trumpet sound?

Task 2 I Asked the Little Boy

5.What is unusual about the coloured things in the poem?

6.What rhyming pattern does the poem have?

7.How does the little boy in the poem use his senses?

8.How does the poem make you feel?

© Pearson Education Ltd 2010. APP for Reading and Writing: Year 4

Task 2 I Asked the Little Boy

Main Assessment Focus: AF2 (understand, describe, select or retrieve information, events or ideas from texts and use quotation and reference to text)

Question	Exemplified responses	Grid reference	Notes
In the poem, what is yellow like?	Quotes from poem: 'Yellow is like something soft and warm.'	Level 3 / bullet 2	
	Identifies from text and comments: 'Something soft and warm, like sunshine / like fur.'	Level 4 / bullet 2	
What colour must be like a thunderstorm?	Quotes from poem: 'Purple.'	Level 3 / bullet 2	
	Identifies from text and comments: 'Purple. It must be like dark clouds or a purple sky.'	Level 4 / bullet 2	

Main Assessment Focus: AF3 (deduce, infer or interpret information, events or ideas from texts)

Question	Exemplified responses	Grid reference	Notes
What is unusual about the coloured things in the poem?	Response based on personal speculation: 'They are all outdoors / in the countryside.'	Level 3 / bullet 2	
	Correctly infers from the text: 'The boy can't see them. He might have been able to see once, and remembers things like green trees or a purple sky.' 'You can hear, smell or feel them.'	Level 4 / bullet 2	
How does the little boy in the poem use his senses?	Straightforward inference: 'He tries to see colours / talks about colours he can't see.'	Level 3 / bullet 1	
	Inference based on the text: 'He uses hearing, smell and touch, because he can't see.'	Level 4 / bullet 1	

Main Assessment Focus: AF5 (explain and comment on writers' use of language, including grammatical and literary features at word and sentence level)

Question	Exemplified responses	Grid reference	Notes
Choose another simile from the poem and explain the comparison.	Identifies a simile with little comment: 'Some roses are pink.'	Level 3	
	Identifies and comments: 'Pink is a pretty colour and roses have a lovely smell.'	Level 4 / bullet 2	
What makes red a good colour for a trumpet sound?	Basic explanation: 'Red is bright.'	Level 3	
	Simple comments on poet's choices: 'It's a bright / lively colour for a loud / lively sound.'	Level 4 / bullet 2	

Other Assessment Focus: AF4 (identify and comment on the structure and organisation of texts, including grammatical and presentational features at text level)

Question	Exemplified responses	Grid reference	Notes
What rhyming pattern does the poem have?	Identifies a few pairs of rhyming lines. Might add comments: '"Think" rhymes with "pink".'	Level 3	
	Identifies the pattern of the whole poem: 'The first line rhymes with the third one – see and he, then they go in twos, but the last two don't rhyme.'	Level 4 / bullet 1	

Other Assessment Focus: AF6 (identify and comment on the overall effect of the text on the reader)

Question	Exemplified responses	Grid reference	Notes
How does the poem make you feel?	Simple personal comment: 'happy', 'sad'. Might add own reason: 'because the boy can't see'.	Level 3 / bullet 2	
	Comment on overall effect on reader: 'Green / rustle of the wind makes me happy.'	Level 4 / bullet 3	

Exemplified responses matched to levels of attainment are provided as a guide. As always, professional judgement must be used when assessing pupils' learning progression and a range of evidence should be gathered for each AF.

Task 2 I Asked the Little Boy

1. Make up some similes for these colours:

   Black is like ....

   Orange is like ....

   Brown is like ....

   Grey is like ....

2. Write some colour similes for these:

   Waves ....

   Seabirds ....

   Sunshine ....

3. Think of a scene for your own similes poem. What can you see, hear, feel and smell? Make notes here.

   See: ....

   ....

   Hear: ....

   ....

   Feel: ....

   ....

   Smell: ....

   ....

4. Now write your poem on a separate sheet of paper.

   REMEMBER!
   • Use descriptive adjectives.
   • Compare things to other things.

Task 2 I Asked the Little Boy

A pupil response within the range for Level 3 might be:

Question 1 (AF7)
- Simple comparisons / similes: e.g. Black is like witches, Orange is like flames, Brown is like mud, Grey is like dark clouds.

Question 2 (AF7)
- Mainly simple vocabulary but includes some words chosen for effect: e.g. Blue is like waves in the sea, White is like seabirds, Yellow is like bright sunshine.

Question 3 (AF1)
- Chooses appropriate scene and gives at least one idea for each of what can be seen, heard, felt and smelled.

Question 4 (AF1, AF5, AF7, AF8)

AF1

The content is appropriate, with some ideas that evoke images of the harbour, although some similes are used just for the sake of the simile.

An imaginative theme for some of the similes: based on food.

There is an attempt to elaborate through clauses: '…my tuna sandwich I had for lunch'; '…tangerine I ate with my tuna sandwich'.

AF5

Varied beginning to first sentence to set the scene ('At Poole harbour…'), but otherwise sentence structure is the same throughout, creating an appropriate pattern for the poem.

Maintains appropriate use of the past tense throughout.

AF7

The vocabulary is simple but appropriate and there is evidence of words chosen for effect: 'a thousand crazy parrots squawking'.

AF8

Simple grammatical function, lexical and content words are spelled correctly, including compound words: 'lifeboat', 'seagulls'.

Content words with more than one morpheme are spelled correctly: 'thousand', 'porridge'.

There is a phonetically plausible attempt at spelling 'squawking'.

Poole Harbour

At poole harbour it smelt as fishy as my tuna sandwich I had for lunch yesterday.

I heard seagulls as loud as a thousand CRAZY parrots squaking at once.

I felt rough stones as lumpy as my porridge.

I saw an RNLI lifeboat as orange as the fresh tangerine I ate with my tuna sanwich.

Task 2 I Asked the Little Boy

A pupil response within the range for Level 4 might be:

Question 1 (AF7)

- Some choices match style of stimulus text: e.g. Black is like witches in long robes, Orange is like flames dancing in a fire, Brown is like a dirty puddle in the mud.

Question 2 (AF7)

- Some words chosen to create the effect of the subject. Might be influenced by the text: e.g. Blue is like waves lapping on a beach, White is like the sound of seabirds whirling in the sky, Yellow is like feeling warm sunshine on my face.

Question 3 (AF1)

- Chooses an imaginative scene and thinks of interesting and appropriate ideas for what can be seen, heard, felt and smelled in that scene.

Question 4 (AF1, AF5, AF7, AF8)

AF1

The content and ideas are relevant, with some evocative similes developed with expanded noun phrases: '100 easter chicks altogether'.

The writer introduces the idea of the sounds, movement and colour of the garden and maintains this throughout.

AF5

There is variation in sentence length and subject as appropriate for a poem.

In keeping with the model 'simile' poem, the main connectives used are 'as' and 'like'.

AF7

The writer has made some deliberate choices of vocabulary to create effects: 'orange trumpets blasting out', 'scrambles... like a rocket'.

There is evidence of vocabulary expansion: 'underfoot'.

AF8

Grammatical function, lexical and content words are spelled correctly, including words with multiple morphemes, inflected endings and compound words: 'lovely', 'colourful', 'sunshine', 'chirping', 'louder', 'daffodils', 'underfoot'.

> **My Garden**
>
> In my garden I can smell roses as sweet as sugar.
> The lovely fresh smell of fir trees, like my bubble bath.
> I can see flower beds as colourful as a rainbow.
> Yellow daffodils shining in the sun, their orange trumpets blasting out.
> I can hear birds chirping louder than 100 easter chicks altogether.
> The rustling of a fox as he scrambles through the bushes like a rocket.
> I can feel hot summer sunshine as warm as a log fire.
> Underfoot the grass tickles my feet like a feather duster

APP for Reading and Writing: Year 4

Task 2 I Asked the Little Boy

Reading

Next steps for developing AF2

Children will benefit from further practice in answering questions that require them to identify, understand and describe ideas in a poem, for example:

- What or who is the poem about?
- What is the setting for the poem?
- How does the poet describe…?

This activity should be part of a range of evidence gathered for AF2 which could also come from sources, such as:

- observations during shared and guided reading of poems;
- children's performances of poems;
- discussions following listening to recordings of poetry, including poets reading their own work.

All tasks in this book provide opportunities to gather evidence for AF2.

Next steps for developing AF3

Children will benefit from further practice in answering inferential questions and using reference to the text to support answers. Useful questions you could ask when reading poems together might be:

- What is the mood of this poem?
- What pictures does the poem make you see in your mind?
- Which line / verse suggests that…?

This activity should be part of a range of evidence gathered for AF3. Evidence for AF3 can be gathered from various sources, such as:

- observations during guided and shared reading of poetry;
- comparing poems with similar themes;
- writing thought bubbles;
- whenever children need to read between the lines in a text (especially a poem, rhyme or verse) in another subject area: e.g. history, RE or PSHE.

Task 1 on pages 8 to 18, Task 3 on pages 29 to 38, Task 4 on pages 39 to 49 and Task 5 on pages 50 to 61 provide other opportunities to gather evidence for AF3.

Next steps for developing AF5

Children will benefit from further practice in answering questions which comment on and explain the writer's use of language. Useful questions you could ask when reading poetry together might be:

- Find three adjectives that describe… What makes them good choices to describe…?
- Find a simile. Explain why the poet has chosen those words.
- Which words does the poet use to describe feelings?
- Which words or phrases produce a sound effect? Why do you think they do?

These activities should be part of a range of evidence gathered for AF5. Evidence can be gathered from a range of sources, such as:

- playing word games, e.g. changing adjectives, verbs and adverbs;
- singing songs and responding to their lyrical meanings and language;
- highlighting a variety of texts to identify words used for different effects;
- using a thesaurus to find synonyms for words such as sad, happy, nice, good.

All tasks in this book provide opportunities to gather evidence for AF5.

Task 2 I Asked the Little Boy

Writing

Next steps for developing AF1

You could develop a thoughtful approach in the children and help them to use their imagination to think up ideas for the content and to create evocative images in poetry. The following discussion points and activities will help:

- Spending time using the senses and listing the things they can see, hear, smell and feel in contrasting settings, then describing these and talking about their effects: quiet, lively, exciting, dreary, dull and so on.
- Thinking about a location they have visited and describing it to a partner: perhaps interviewing one another to elicit opinions.
- Compiling word-banks of expressive words and phrases, including similes.
- Discussing the effectiveness of similes they have used: e.g. 'as lumpy as the porridge…'. How is lumpy porridge different from stones? (It is soft, not hard, so perhaps a harder-sounding simile would be better.)

This should be part of a range of writing activities from which evidence is gathered for AF1. Evidence for AF1 can also be gathered from:

- generating ideas for writing other poetry as well as narrative texts;
- generating ideas for writing non-fiction.

Task 1 on pages 8 to 18, Task 4 on pages 39 to 49, Task 5 on pages 50 to 61 and Task 6 on pages 62 to 71 also provide opportunities to gather evidence for AF1.

Next steps for developing AF7

You could develop the children's vocabulary and their appreciation of the effects of words through activities and discussions such as:

- Picking out effective words from their writing and talking about their effects: e.g. 'a thousand crazy parrots squawking' makes use of alliteration of the 's' and 'z' sounds and the onomatopoeia of 'squawking'; 'orange trumpets blasting' creates a powerful effect of daffodils bursting out of their buds through the use of the powerful verb 'blasting'.
- Asking if they can think of better words, phrases or sentences than one or two of those they used: e.g. 'scramble… like a rocket' (Rockets do not scramble – the movement is much more linear and powerful, also foxes do not really scramble – they creep through bushes). A better image might be 'creeping through the bushes like a spy'.
- Reading their poems aloud and considering their effects, then deciding whether the effect is right.

This should be part of a range of writing activities from which evidence is gathered for AF7. Evidence for AF7 can also be gathered from:

- word lists connected with topics the children have studied in other subjects, especially science or geography;
- previous work on the connotations of words;
- brainstorming words connected with sensory experiences.

Task 4 on pages 39 to 49, Task 5 on pages 50 to 61 and Task 6 on pages 62 to 71 provide other opportunities to gather evidence for AF7.

Task 3 How Does It Work?

Aims of this task

This task is designed to help you to make judgements about children's attainment in Reading **AF4, AF5** and **AF6** (with opportunities to assess **AF1, AF2** and **AF3** as well) and Writing **AF2, AF5** and **AF6** (with opportunities to assess **AF3** and **AF8** as well). The children read and respond to a non-fiction explanation text describing how a vacuum cleaner works. The children write their own explanation texts on how a pencil sharpener works.

Related Renewed Framework unit

Non-fiction Unit 3: Explanation texts

Renewed Framework objectives

7.2, 7.4, 9.1, 10.1, 10.2

Key concepts

Reading

- find specific information in the explanation text (AF2)
- identify and explain features of the layout, organisation and illustration of the text (AF4)
- comment on the writer's use of interesting language (AF5)
- identify and comment on the purpose of the explanation text (AF6)

Writing

- write an explanation text which explains how a pencil sharpener works (AF2, AF6)
- write notes using the present tense (AF5)

Questions for guided reading

Starting off

Ask what type of text this is. The children could talk about other explanations they have read. Ask them to read it (AF1) and to notice how well it explains how a vacuum cleaner works and how interesting they find it.

Read and respond

Use the following questions as part of a group discussion:

- **What is this text for? (AF6)**
- **What is a vacuum cleaner powered by? (AF2)**
- **Why doesn't the dust escape with the air? (AF3)**
- **How does the diagram help to explain why the dust doesn't escape? (AF4)**
- **How do other parts of the layout help? (AF4)**
- **Which words help to make the explanation inviting to a reader? (AF5)**
- **How does the writer use a comparison to help the explanation? (AF5)**

Going deeper

- **How does the writer use punctuation and different types of print to make the explanation exciting and interesting? (AF5)**
- **Which connecting words in the text are often used for explaining something? (AF5)**

Reflect

Discuss how successful the explanation is. Do the children now understand how a vacuum cleaner works? Can they explain it without looking at the page? (AF6)

Task 3 How Does It Work?

Dudley showed me how a vacuum cleaner works.

1 Vacuum cleaners are powered by a mini **motor** that runs on electricity. So, before switching it on, it needs to be plugged into a nearby socket.

2 WHIRRRR! Once the motor is running, it turns a fan round and round. As the fan spins, it pushes air out of the vacuum cleaner through a tube called a **duct**.

3 Because air is pushed out of the cleaner, air gets sucked in through the **head** to take its place, just like water being sucked up through a straw.

4 And as the air gets sucked up through the **hose**, so does the dirt and dust.

5 SSLLUUUUP! All this dust is then sucked up into a **bag**. But where does all the air go? It escapes through tiny holes in the walls of the bag. The dirt and dust are trapped inside – they're too big to get through the holes.

6 The bag fills up and after a while needs emptying or replacing. If you don't keep an eye on it, it becomes so full that it …

BURSTS!

Head – this is attached to the **hose**.

Duct

Electric motor

Dust bag

Air gets sucked in here.

Task 3 How Does It Work?

1. What is this text for?

2. What is a vacuum cleaner powered by?

3. Why doesn't the dust escape with the air?

4. How does the diagram help to explain why the dust doesn't escape?

5. How do other parts of the layout help?

Task 3 How Does It Work?

6. Which words help to make the explanation inviting to a reader?

7. How does the writer use a comparison to help the explanation?

8. How does the writer use punctuation and different types of print to make the explanation exciting and interesting?

9. Which connecting words in the text are often used for explaining something?

Task 3 How Does It Work?

Main Assessment Focus: AF4 (identify and comment on the structure and organisation of texts, including grammatical and presentational features at text level)

Question	Exemplified responses	Grid reference	Notes
How does the diagram help to explain why the dust doesn't escape?	Identifies basic feature: 'It shows where everything fits together.'	Level 3	
	Interprets diagram: 'It shows where the air and dust go in and how the air gets out but the dust stays in.'	Level 4 / bullet 2	
How do other parts of the layout help?	Identifies a few basic features: 'The numbers show what happens first and what happens next. The labels tell you where the motor / bag / duct / head / hose is.'	Level 3	
	Identifies and comments on a number of features: 'Heading says what it's about'; 'Separate paragraphs make it easy to read about each part'; 'Numbers in text show the order it all happens in'.	Level 4 / bullet 2	

Main Assessment Focus: AF5 (explain and comment on writers' use of language, including grammatical and literary features at word and sentence level)

Question	Exemplified responses	Grid reference	Notes
Which words help to make the explanation inviting to a reader?	Identifies writer's choices: 'BURSTS! WHIRR! SSLLUUUP! They sound funny / good.'	Level 3	
	Comments on writer's choices: 'WHIRR! SSLLUUUP! Sound like a vacuum cleaner / sound exciting / fun.'	Level 4 / bullet 2	
How does the writer use punctuation to make the explanation exciting and interesting?	Identifies choices with some comment: 'Exclamation marks make it sound exciting.'	Level 3	
	Identifies and comments on writer's choices: 'Words in bold make you look for them in the diagram'; 'A question makes you think about what happens'.	Level 4 / bullet 1	

Main Assessment Focus: AF6 (identify and comment on writers' purposes and viewpoints, and the overall effect of the text on the reader)

Question	Exemplified responses	Grid reference	Notes
What is this text for?	Identifies main purpose: 'To explain / show you how a vacuum cleaner works.'	Level 3 / bullet 1	
	Identifies main purpose and comments: 'Shows what happens inside, tells you the names of all the parts.'	Level 4 / bullet 1	

Other Assessment Focus: AF2 (understand, describe, select or retrieve information, events or ideas from texts and use quotation and reference to text)

Question	Exemplified responses	Grid reference	Notes
What is a vacuum cleaner powered by?	Simple points identified: 'A mini motor.'	Level 3 / bullet 1	
	Some relevant points identified: 'A mini motor which runs on electricity.'	Level 4 / bullet 1	

Other Assessment Focus: AF3 (deduce, infer or interpret information, events or ideas from texts)

Question	Exemplified responses	Grid reference	Notes
Why doesn't the dust escape with the air?	Inference on single point in text: 'It doesn't fit through the little holes. Only air fits through the little holes.'	Level 3 / bullet 1	
	Inference based on different points including the diagram: 'The air gets through the holes in the bag but the bits of dust are too big to get through.' Might comment: 'like a sieve', 'like a filter'.	Level 4 / bullet 1	

Exemplified responses matched to levels of attainment are provided as a guide. As always, professional judgement must be used when assessing pupils' learning progression and a range of evidence should be gathered for each AF.

Task 3 How Does It Work?

1. Explain how a pencil sharpener works. Write notes in the boxes to say what each part does.

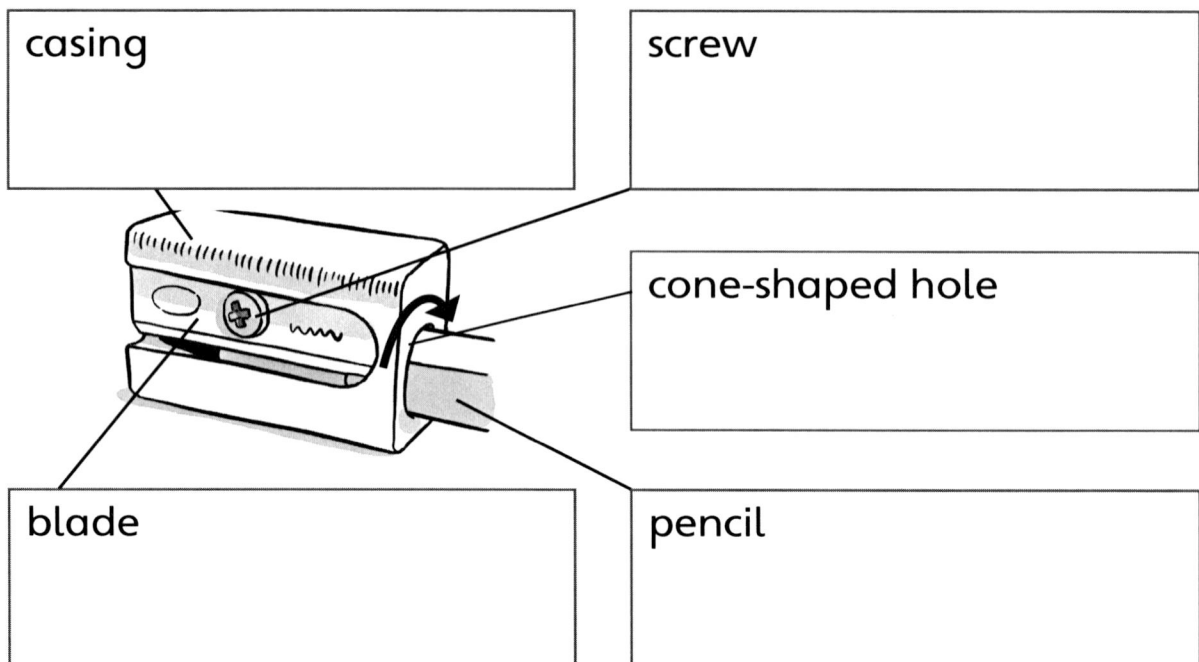

casing

screw

cone-shaped hole

blade

pencil

2. Imagine some aliens looking at a pencil sharpener. Explain to them what it is for.

3. Write a sentence to introduce an explanation of how a pencil sharpener works.

4. Finish your explanation about how a pencil sharpener works. Write on another sheet of paper.

REMEMBER!
- Start a new paragraph for each part of the explanation.
- Use the present tense.
- Use connecting words that help to explain.

© Pearson Education Ltd 2010. APP for Reading and Writing: Year 4

Task 3 How Does It Work?

A pupil response within the range for Level 3 might be:

Question 1 (AF5)

- Writes mainly in note form but might lapse into prose; mainly present tense.

Question 2 (AF5, AF6)

- Present tense; mainly accurate full stops and capital letters; mainly simple sentences, but might use a complex sentence (clauses with subordination): e.g. 'It is for making a point on a pencil, and then the pencil can write'; or 'You use it to make a point on a pencil so you can write with it or draw.'

Question 3 (AF5, AF6)

- Sentence in present tense. Makes sense, with full stop and capital letter.

Question 4 (AF2, AF3, AF5, AF6, AF8)

AF2

The main purpose is established at a general level, but content is sparse. Heading (How It Works?) does not clearly state purpose.

AF3

There is some attempt to organise ideas with the opening clearly signalled, stating what the text is about.

The closing is signalled as a simple summary.

There is some attempt at sequencing, but not clearly signalled, with no step-by-step explanation.

> How It works?
>
> A Pencil sharkener works by it making a blade inside a plastic casing. The way it makes your pencil sharp is the blade takes off layers of wood so the led is sharp.
>
> You need to turn your pencil so it cuts the wood to the same amount on each side so it work properly and is easy to use.

AF5

Complex sentences are used but the structure is insecure: '...works by it having...'.

The main connectives are 'and' and 'so', with over-use of 'so'.

Use of the present tense is consistent and appropriate for the purpose.

AF6

Sentences are accurately demarcated by capital letters and full stops.

AF8

Grammatical function words, content and lexical words are mainly correctly spelled: 'inside', 'of', 'off', 'sharp', 'sharpener', 'pencil'.

There is a phonetically plausible attempt to spell 'lead' ('led').

Task 3 How Does It Work?

A pupil response within the range for Level 4 might be:

Questions 1 (AF5)

- Uses note form with logical connectives: 'so', 'so that', 'when'. Consistent use of present tense.

Question 2 (AF5, AF6)

- Use of complex sentences with more use of commas to mark clauses (may not be in correct places): e.g. 'It is for shaving some wood off a pencil, so that lead shows at the end, and it makes a point, so you can write or draw with it.'

Question 3 (AF5, AF6)

- As above: e.g. 'A pencil sharpener works by shaving a thin layer off the pencil, in a spiral that can go on and on.'

Question 4 (AF2, AF3, AF5, AF6, AF8)

AF2

The main purpose is clear (although the heading does not clearly state it, using 'it' rather than 'a pencil sharpener') and the main features of the form are used (the explanation is split into numbered paragraphs).

Awareness of the reader is shown through the use of 'you'.

AF3

The writer clusters ideas according to the function of each part of the pencil sharpener.

There is a fitting opening ('Pencil sharpeners are used in everyday life'), but the closing is abrupt.

The ideas are logically sequenced, mentioning each part in the sequence in which it is used, beginning with the hole into which the pencil is placed and ending with the blade slicing away the wood.

AF5

Sentence lengths and structures are varied, with some simple and some complex sentences.

Subordinating connectives are used: 'to', 'which', 'so that', 'when', 'where'.

The main tense, appropriately for an explanation, is the present, with correct use of the future.

AF6

Sentences are demarcated accurately throughout with capital letters and full stops, also commas to mark clauses.

AF8

Grammatical function, regularly spelled content / lexical words (including multiple morphemes) and present and past tense inflections are mainly correctly spelled.

The only mistake is 'theirselves' (for 'themselves') – spelled 'thereselves'.

How does it work?

1. Pencil sharpeners are used in everyday life to stop pencils from becoming blunt. What happens is there is a little blade inside a plastic or metal case which makes it easier to hold eg and st stops people from cutting themselves.

2. There is a cone shaped hole which you p you place your pencil in. That will keep it in place place so that when you rotate the pencil, the blade will slice it carefully.

3. There is a screw which keeps the blade nice and secure.

4. The blade is in a position where, when the pencil rotates, the blade can easily slice away the wood.

Task 3 How Does It Work?

Reading

Next steps for developing AF4

Children will benefit from further practice in answering questions about the structure of explanations. Discussion points and questions like the following will help:

• What do you notice about how the text is set out?
• How does this help you to understand how... works?
• How does the writer use the layout to make it easier to...?
• What different types of font can you find?
• Why does the writer use these?

This activity should be part of a range of evidence gathered for AF4. Other evidence for AF4 can come from sources, such as:

• discussions of other non-fiction texts, including leaflets and directions;
• discussions of visuals from informative television programmes;
• guided and shared reading of screen layouts of websites.

Task 2 on pages 19 to 28, Task 5 on pages 50 to 61 and Task 6 on pages 62 to 71 provide other opportunities to gather evidence for AF4.

Next steps for developing AF5

Children will benefit from further practice in answering questions about language and grammatical features and identifying these in texts, for example:

• Find some technical words. How does the writer explain what they mean?
• Which words are used to add interest?
• Which word helps you to understand...?
• Why does the writer use questions in this explanation?

This activity should be part of a range of evidence gathered for AF5. Evidence for AF5 can be gathered from various sources, such as:

• observations about explanations in other subjects (e.g. science);
• recapping explanations, with reference to a diagram, if necessary;
• when children present what they have learned to the rest of the class / group.

All tasks in this book provide opportunities to gather evidence for AF5.

Next steps for developing AF6

You could develop the children's understanding of writers' viewpoints and purposes through discussion points such as:

• What was this text written for?
• How well does it explain?
• How does the writer want readers to respond?

This activity should be part of a range of evidence gathered for AF6 which could also come from sources, such as:

• reading a variety of different explanation texts from different media (e.g. print, online, television) and identifying their audiences and purposes;
• evaluating the effectiveness of explanation texts read;
• role-play activities in which pairs take turns to be listener and explainer.

Task 2 on pages 19 to 28, Task 4 on pages 39 to 49, and Task 6 on pages 62 to 71 provide other opportunities to gather evidence for AF6.

Task 3 How Does It Work?

Writing

Next steps for developing AF2

The children will benefit from questions and activities that encourage them to think about the purpose for which an explanation is written and who will read it, such as:

- What are you explaining?
- Enact the process (e.g. sharpening a pencil), use 'freeze frames' and talk through each stage, saying which part is in use and what it does.
- Write notes about each stage and then fill them out to write sentences.

This should be part of a range of writing activities from which evidence is gathered for AF2. Evidence for AF2 can also be gathered from:

- writing other non-fiction texts for a specific audience: e.g. news recounts or reports for people interested in a specific topic (e.g. science, sports, fashion);
- writing narrative texts for specific age groups.

Task 5 on pages 50 to 61 and Task 6 on pages 62 to 71 provide other opportunities to gather evidence for AF2.

Next steps for developing AF5

You could develop the children's skills in writing appropriate types of sentence to make explanations clear and concise, and interesting to the reader, through discussion points and activities such as:

- Looking at the first words of each sentence in an explanation and considering whether they are repetitive.
- Removing unnecessary words from sentences or shortening them in other ways: e.g. 'This is how a pencil sharpener works. It has a blade in a plastic casing.'
- Rearranging long sentences to find the best order for phrases and clauses: e.g. where is the best for the clause 'when the pencil rotates'?

This should be part of a range of writing activities from which evidence is gathered for AF5. Evidence for AF5 can also be gathered from:

- sentences the children write in other subjects, to communicate information, ideas or points of view;
- writing notes and then filling them out to create sentences.

Task 1 on pages 8 to 18, Task 2 on pages 19 to 28 and Task 4 on pages 39 to 49 provide other opportunities to gather evidence for AF5.

Next steps for developing AF6

You could develop the children's understanding of syntax, punctuation and sentence structure in explanations through the following:

- Reading one another's writing and looking for missing punctuation. How does this help the reader to make sense of the writing?
- Adding details to sentences through extra clauses that are marked by commas.

This should be part of a range of writing activities from which evidence is gathered for AF6. Evidence for AF6 can also be gathered from:

- other narrative writing where punctuation is important for meaning or effect;
- non-fiction writing that includes phrases and clauses linked by time or logical connectives, and finding alternative connectives to avoid repetition;
- transcribing a short dialogue, using speech marks to make clear what is said and by whom.

Task 1 on pages 8 to 18 and Task 5 on pages 50 to 61 provide other opportunities to gather evidence for AF6.

Task 4 The Thief in Ash Road School

Aims of this task

This task is designed to help you to make judgements about children's attainment in Reading **AF3, AF5** and **AF6** (with opportunities to assess AF1 and AF2 as well) and Writing **AF1, AF3** and **AF4** (with opportunities to assess AF5, AF7 and AF8 as well). The children read and respond to an extract from a story set in a school and in which one pupil faces a difficult dilemma. The children write their own story with a dilemma.

Related Renewed Framework unit

Narrative Unit 4: Stories that raise dilemmas

Renewed Framework objectives

7.1, 7.2, 8.2, 9.1, 11.1

Key concepts

Reading

- deduce information and events by 'reading between the lines' (AF3)
- identify words and phrases that communicate how a character feels (AF5)
- identify the author's message in the story (AF6)

Writing

- write a story based on a dilemma (AF1)
- plan the main events in paragraphs, making notes about how the problem will be resolved and how the story might end (AF3)
- write in paragraphs and use cohesion between them (AF4)

Questions for guided reading

Starting off

Ask if the children know what is meant by a 'dilemma'. They could give examples. Discuss why someone facing a dilemma might not want to do what they feel is right. What affects their decision? Ask them to read the story (AF1) and to notice who faces a dilemma, and what it is.

Read and respond

Use the following questions as part of a group discussion:

- **Who faced a dilemma and what was the dilemma? (AF2)**
- **Why didn't Jamie want to tell Miss Andrews what he had seen? (AF3)**
- **Why couldn't Jamie do his work? (AF3)**
- **What was Ryan Fisk like? (AF3)**
- **Which words make you feel Jamie's worry before he told Miss Andrews about Ryan? (AF5)**
- **Which words and phrases show how Jamie felt after school? (AF5)**

Going deeper

- **What is the message of this story? (AF6)**
- **Did Ryan steal the phone? Explain your answer. (AF3)**

Reflect

Discuss whether Jamie did the right thing and whether this was what the children expected him to do. (AF3) They could also comment on how realistic the story is and explain their answers. (AF6)

Task 4 The Thief in Ash Road School
by Jenny Alexander

Megan's mobile phone has gone missing during morning playtime. Someone must have taken it, but no one has owned up. One boy in the class, Jamie, has seen something but doesn't know what to do for the best…

At lunch time, when the class left the room, Jamie stayed back.

"Is everything all right, Jamie?" Miss Andrews asked.

Jamie looked at her and then said reluctantly, "I think I know who took Megan's phone. I saw him coming out of our classroom at playtime – but he'll kill me if he finds out I told you."

"Then we must make sure he doesn't find out," said Miss Andrews. "I can just tell the headteacher that this person was seen in my classroom – there's no need for me to say who saw him."

Jamie didn't know if he could trust Miss Andrews because she might not know how important it was. He didn't think teachers could really understand how scary someone like Ryan Fisk could be. But it was too late to turn back.

"It was Ryan Fisk,' he whispered.

Task 4 The Thief in Ash Road School
by Jenny Alexander

The next day Jamie couldn't do his work. He kept looking at the door waiting. Ryan might come looking for him. Then, just before home time, the door suddenly opened and Mrs Flint, the headteacher, came in with Megan's phone.

So he was right! It was Ryan who stole the phone. But did Ryan know who had told on him?

To his horror, Jamie saw Ryan sitting outside Mrs Flint's office after school and he had to walk right past him. Jamie's heart was pounding and his hands felt clammy, but Ryan hardly even looked at him.

That was when Jamie knew that Miss Andrews had kept her word and was glad that he had helped to catch the thief in Ash Road School.

Task 4 The Thief in Ash Road School

1. Who faced a dilemma and what was the dilemma?

2. Why didn't Jamie want to tell Miss Andrews what he had seen?

3. Why couldn't Jamie do his work?

4. What was Ryan Fisk like?

Task 4 The Thief in Ash Road School

5. Which words make you feel Jamie's worry before he told Miss Andrews about Ryan?

6. Which words and phrases show how Jamie felt after school?

7. What is the message of this story?

8. Did Ryan steal the phone? Explain your answer.

Task 4 The Thief in Ash Road School

Main Assessment Focus: AF3 (deduce, infer or interpret information, events or ideas from texts)

Question	Exemplified responses	Grid reference	Notes
Why didn't Jamie want to tell Miss Andrews what he had seen?	Straightforward inference: 'He was scared because it says Ryan would kill him.'	Level 3 / bullet 1	
	Inference from different points: 'Ryan would hurt him. He said "he'll kill me" ' 'He kept looking at the door scared in case Ryan came looking for him.'	Level 4 / bullet 1	
What was Ryan Fisk like?	Straightforward inference: 'A bully. Jamie said he would kill him if he found out he had told on him.'	Level 3 / bullet 1	
	Inference from different points: 'A thief – he stole a phone'; 'Tough – Jamie was scared of him; it said Jamie thought he was scary.'	Level 4 / bullet 1	
Did Ryan steal the phone? Explain your answer.	Straightforward inference: 'Yes. It says it was Ryan who stole the phone.'	Level 3 / bullet 1	
	Inference from different points: 'Yes because Jamie saw him in the classroom'; 'Mrs Flint came in with the phone and it says "Jamie was right. It was Ryan who stole the phone".'	Level 4 / bullet 1	

Main Assessment Focus: AF5 (explain and comment on writers' use of language, including grammatical and literary features at word and sentence level)

Which words make you feel Jamie's worry before he told Miss Andrews about Ryan?	Identifies words: 'Reluctantly, scary, whispered.'	Level 3	
	Simple comments on choices: 'Reluctantly – it means he didn't want to'; 'Whispered – he whispered because he was scared to say Ryan's name'; 'Scary – it says Ryan was scary.'	Level 4 / bullet 2	
Which words and phrases show how Jamie felt after school?	Identifies words and phrases: 'Jamie's heart was pounding, clammy.' Might also include words from earlier in the day: scary, whispered.	Level 3	
	Simple comments on choices: '"To his horror, Jamie's heart was pounding, his hands felt clammy." This make you think he was scared to walk past Ryan.'	Level 4 / bullet 2	

Main Assessment Focus: AF6 (identify and comment on writers' purposes and viewpoints, and the overall effect of the text on the reader)

What is the message of this story?	Comments identify main purpose: 'You should tell a teacher if you see someone doing something bad.'	Level 3 / bullet 1	
	Main purpose identified: 'The story is saying that it's right to tell on someone if they do something wrong. It says Jamie was glad.'	Level 4 / bullet 1	

Other Assessment Focus: AF2 (understand, describe, select or retrieve information, events or ideas from texts and use quotation and references to text)

Who faced a dilemma and what was the dilemma?	Obvious point identified: 'Jamie – he was scared to tell Miss Andrews he had seen Ryan in the classroom.'	Level 3 / bullet 1	
	Main point identified with comments: 'Jamie. He knew he should tell Miss Andrews he had seen Ryan in the classroom (might add 'to help her to get Megan's phone back') but he was scared of Ryan.'	Level 4 / bullet 1	

© Pearson Education Ltd 2010. APP for Reading and Writing: Year 4

Task 4 The Thief in Ash Road School

1. Think about an idea for a story with a dilemma. Write notes about the setting, main character and dilemma.

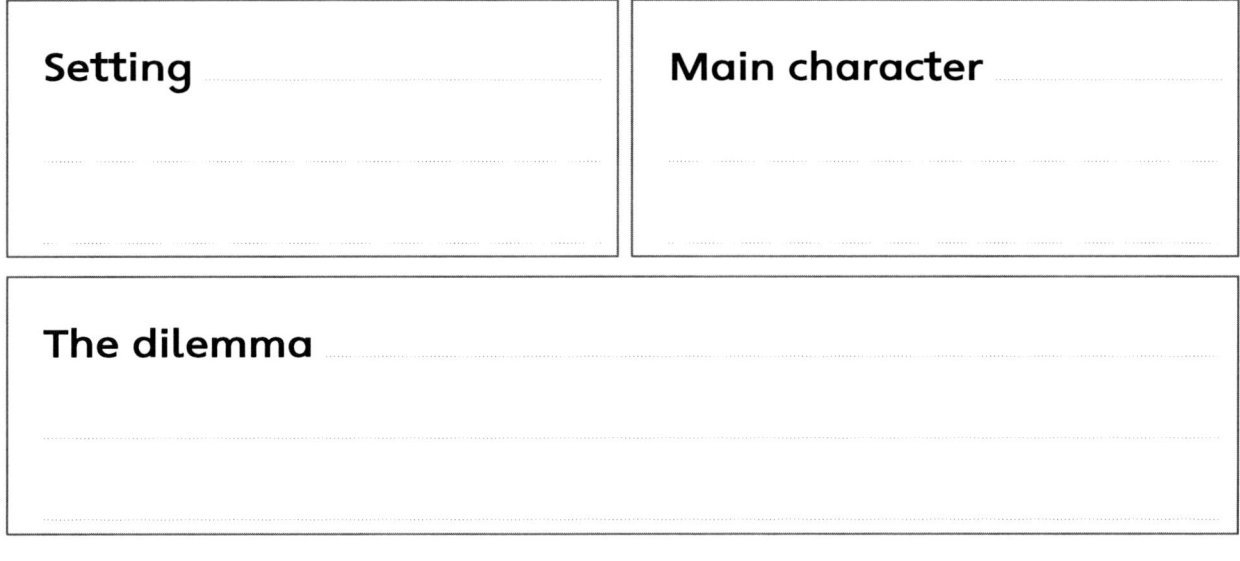

Setting

Main character

The dilemma

2. Plan your story. Write notes for the main events. Use the arrows to write words that might link the paragraphs.

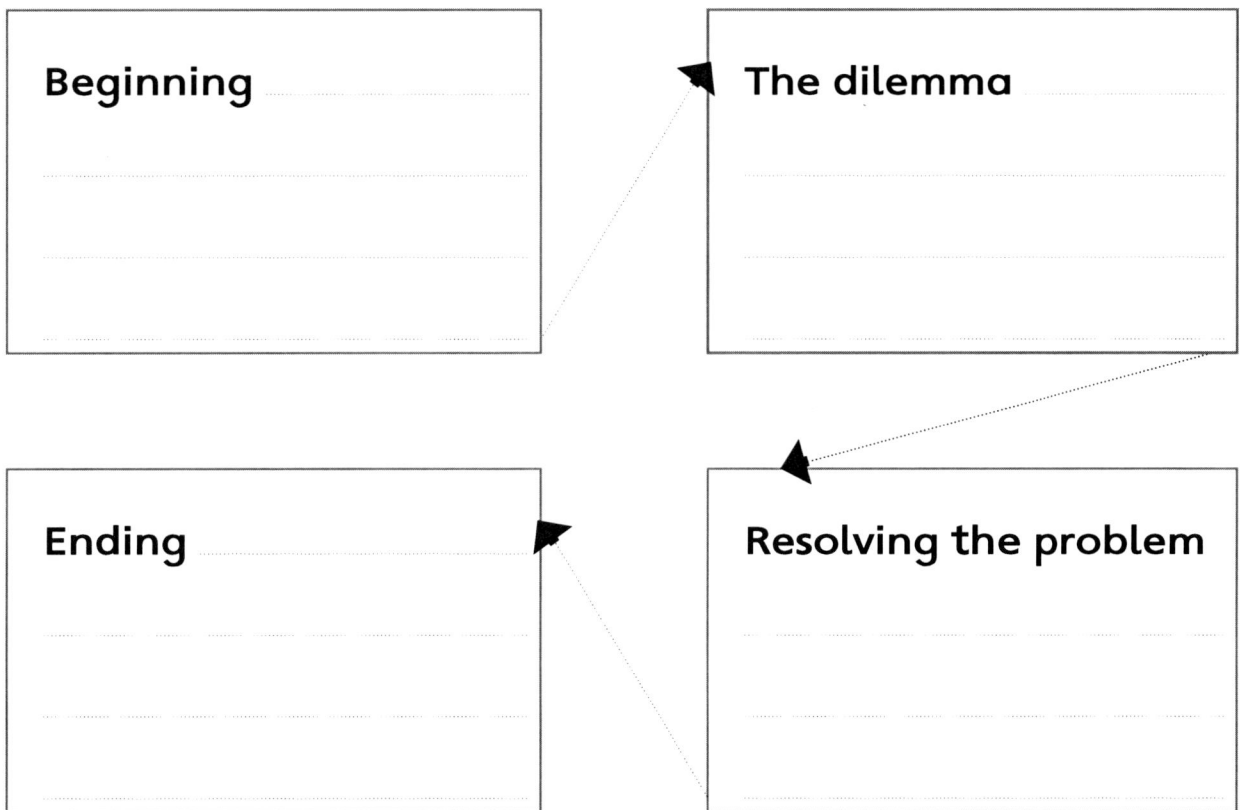

Beginning

The dilemma

Ending

Resolving the problem

3. Write a paragraph or two for the dilemma part of your story on a separate piece of paper.

   REMEMBER! Use interesting words to link your sentences and paragraphs.

Task 4 The Thief in Ash Road School

A pupil response within the range for Level 3 might be:

Question 1 (AF1)
- Develops the dilemma idea in the text either by changing the setting or coming up with a different but familiar dilemma set in a school.

Question 2 (AF3)
- Boxes completed mainly in note form, showing some grasp of the logical sequence of the main events in the story; suggests how the dilemma is resolved and how the story ends.

Question 3 (AF1, AF3, AF4, AF5, AF7, AF8)

AF1
Appropriate ideas and content: shows understanding of what is meant by a dilemma and sets the dilemma in a known context (school) with appropriate characters (football coach and children in the team) and actions.

Some attempt to elaborate: includes the adverb 'accidentally'.

AF3
Opening signalled in a way that sets the scene ('Today...').

Story sequenced logically with Sophia's explanation inserted into the sequence using dialogue.

AF4
Some links between sentences within the paragraph through the use of personal, possessive and reflexive pronouns: 'she', 'her', 'his', 'herself', 'you'.

AF5
Mainly simply-structured sentences.

Common connectives: 'and', 'but'.

Some subordination using connectives: '...until coach said...'

Limited variation in tense (past for narrative, present for dialogue).

AF7
Simple, generally appropriate vocabulary: 'talk tactics', 'football tournament', 'coach'.

Some words / phrases chosen for effect: 'silence hung in the air'.

AF8
Correct spelling of some common grammatical function words: 'well', 'until', 'always'.

Common content / lexical words with more than one morpheme, including compound words: 'football', 'tournament', 'coach'.

Error in inflected ending: past tense ('happend').

Phonetically plausible attempts at content / lexical words: 'tacticks', 'acsidently'.

Dilemma 1

Today was the day of the school football tournament. "Now everyone gather we need to talk tackticks" said coach. "I'm here, I'm so sorry I'm late, I've just come back from the hospital" said Sophia the star-striker "what happend to you" shouted one of her teammates Sophia replied." well I was playing football with my brother and he accidently broke my leg." Silence hung in the air until coach said" you could always pick another player!" She thought about Jack who was her best friend but she also thought about a boy called Phill. "Now Jack always turns up to practice but isn't very good at scoring, but phil is good at scoring but his behaviour is terrible." she thought to herself.

Task 4 The Thief in Ash Road School

A pupil response within the range for Level 4 might be:

Question 1 (AF1)

- Comes up with an idea for a dilemma appropriate for the chosen main character and setting.

Question 2 (AF3)

- Notes show thought about setting the scene, introducing the dilemma, an idea for resolving it and an ending that might give a message.

Question 3 (AF1, AF3, AF4, AF5, AF7, AF8)

AF1

Relevant ideas and content: issues of bullying and racism at school developed in detail, with Zara describing events to the teacher.

Descriptive detail: 'palms were sweaty'.

Use of adverbials: 'amazingly'.

Consistent stance maintained: story told in third person.

An interesting twist to a story modelled on the example: Bob apologising to, instead of ignoring, his victim.

AF3

Ideas organised with a fitting opening and ending: sets the scene, narrates events and ends with the dilemma solved and future situation / events indicated.

AF4

Paragraphs help to organise the story: opening that sets the scene, dialogue that develops the story then narrative that continues the narration, followed by an ending in which the dilemma is resolved.

Bob the Big Bully

Bob, the biggest boy in school is bullying Zara, because of her skin colour. Zara isn't sure if she should tell the teacher or leave it be. If she did tell, she was sure he would bully her more. What should she do?

When everyone went out to play, Zara stayed in.
"Are you alright, Zara?" Miss Peterson asked.
Zara was reluctant but she spoke, "Bob, in class 6 is bullying me because of my skin colour and he's making me really upset. Please don't mention I told you, even though he'll know anyway. He'll kill me after school!"
Miss Peterson paused, "Of course. Don't worry. Everything will be alright. But why didn't you tell me sooner?"
"I was scared." Zara answered, looking at her feet.

Zara paused at the classroom door. It was the end of the day and she knew Miss Peterson had talked to Bob. She had to go past the headteachers office to get out of school and she was nervous.

Her palms were sweaty as she neared the office. Amazingly, when she walked past, Bob said sorry and that he had been rude and wouldn't do it again!

AF5

Variation of sentence lengths (4th paragraph).

Subjects of sentences varied: 'Bob', 'Zara', 'she', 'Miss Peterson', 'he'.

Subordinating connectives throughout the text: 'if', 'even though', 'as', 'when'.

Variation in tense (present used in the opening to set the scene and in dialogue; past in narrative).

Accurate tenses and verb forms.

AF7

Evidence of deliberate vocabulary choices: 'reluctant', 'paused', 'amazingly', 'nervous'.

Avoids repetition using different words to suggest fear / unease: 'reluctant', 'looking at her feet', 'nervous', 'her palms were sweaty'.

AF8

Correct spelling of most common grammatical function words: 'because', 'should', 'would', 'wouldn't', 'anyway'; common content / lexical words with multiple morphemes, including compound words: 'nervous', 'mention', 'palms'.

Past and present tense inflections spelled correctly: 'bullying', 'stayed', 'answered', 'paused', 'neared', 'walked'.

Task 4 The Thief in Ash Road School

Reading

Next steps for developing A3

Children can develop skills in deduction, inference and interpretation of stories and become more adept at supporting these with references to stories through discussion and questioning, for example:

- How did x feel when…?
- Which words in the story make you think that?
- How did x make y feel better? Where does it tell you that?
- How would you feel if…? Did x feel like that? Which words tell you that?

This activity should be part of a range of evidence gathered for AF3. Evidence for AF3 can be gathered from various sources, such as:

- observations during guided and shared reading of different text genres;
- responding to films, broadcasts etc;
- writing thought bubbles for characters in stories;
- reading between the lines in a text in other subjects: e.g. history, RE, PSHE.

Task 1 on pages 8 to 18, Task 2 on pages 19 to 28, Task 3 on pages 29 to 38 and Task 5 on pages 50 to 61 also provide opportunities to gather evidence for AF3.

Next steps for developing AF5

Further practice in answering questions about language and grammatical features will help. Questions and discussion points like those below could be asked during shared or guided reading:

- Look for some good words for 'said'.
- What do you notice about the kinds of words the writer uses for…?
- How does the writer show that x feels scared / lonely / excited?

This activity should be part of a range of evidence gathered for AF5. Evidence for AF5 can be gathered from sources such as:

- discussions of descriptive passages or where a writer creates an atmosphere;
- responding to performance poems, rhymes and jingles;
- commenting on and discussing the connotations of words;
- whenever there are opportunities to think about the effects of words.

All tasks in this book provide opportunities to gather evidence for AF5.

Next steps for developing AF6

You could develop the children's understanding of writers' viewpoints and purposes and the effects of stories on readers through questions such as:

- What does this story make you think about?
- What issue(s) is the story about?
- How does it make you feel about…?
- Do you think x was right to…?

This activity should be part of a range of evidence gathered for AF6 which could also come from sources such as:

- observations during guided and shared reading of stories, poems, films etc with dilemmas or that raise issues;
- drama activities, such as hot-seating and interviewing, where characters' motives and viewpoints are explored;
- writing book reviews.

Task 2 on pages 19 to 28, Task 3 on pages 29 to 38 and Task 6 on pages 62 to 71 provide other opportunities to gather evidence for AF6.

Task 4 The Thief in Ash Road School

Writing

Next steps for developing AF1

You could develop children's ability to use their imagination to make their story-writing appeal to the reader through discussion points and activities such as:

• Citizenship work on issues that can lead to dilemmas at school or at home.
• Creating a 'Problem page' forum, in which children write letters, anonymously, and discuss options together and then write 'What might happen if...' stories.
• Word-banks of expressive words and phrases concerning an issue.

This should be part of a range of writing activities from which evidence is gathered for AF1. Evidence for AF1 can also be gathered from:

• generating ideas for writing other narrative texts and poetry;
• generating ideas for writing non-fiction.

Task 1 on pages 8 to 18, Task 2 on pages 19 to 28, Task 5 on pages 50 to 61 and Task 6 on pages 62 to 71 also provide opportunities to gather evidence for AF1.

Next steps for developing AF3

You could develop the children's understanding of how to organise and present stories through discussion points and activities such as:

• Looking at how they began a story, chapter or paragraph: how it sets the scene for a story or links to a previous chapter or paragraph.
• Listing the key events of a story or chapter in the correct order as a flow-chart.
• How they ended a chapter or story, and why. Did they want to 'tie up all the loose ends', suggest to the reader what might happen in the future?

This should be part of a range of writing activities from which evidence is gathered for AF3. Evidence for AF3 can also be gathered from:

• planning, organising and writing other genres of narrative text;
• planning, organising and writing poetry;
• planning, organising and writing non-fiction texts.

Task 1 on pages 8 to 18, Task 3 on pages 29 to 38 and Task 6 on pages 62 to 71 provide other opportunities to gather evidence for AF3.

Next steps for developing AF4

You could develop the children's skills in constructing and linking paragraphs and connecting sentences within paragraphs through:

• Cutting up and reordering sentences of a paragraph from a published story.
• Deleting connectives from a published paragraph and asking the children to suggest what the missing words and phrases might be.
• Deleting short sentences, exclamations and so on that link to other paragraphs and asking the children to discuss how to fill the gaps.

This should be part of a range of writing activities from which evidence is gathered for AF4. Evidence for AF4 can also be gathered from:

• writing other narrative texts;
• writing non-fiction texts, including formal and informal letters.

Task 1 on pages 8 to 18 and Task 6 on pages 62 to 71 provide other opportunities to gather evidence for AF4.

Task 5 The Second Legion

Aims of this task

This task is designed to help you to make judgements about children's attainment in Reading **AF4**, **AF5** and **AF7** (with opportunities to assess AF1, AF2 and AF3 as well) and Writing **AF2**, **AF6** and **AF7** (with opportunities to assess AF1 and AF8 as well). The children read and respond to a passage from a playscript set in Roman Britain and depicting Roman soldiers preparing for battle. The children write their own playscript for another scene.

Related Renewed Framework unit

Narrative Unit 5: Plays (also Narrative Unit 1: Stories with historical settings)

Renewed Framework objectives

7. 1, 7.2, 7.3, 7.4, 9.2, 9.5

Key concepts
Reading
• deduce what characters in the play are like (AF3)
• comment on how the writer structures and organises the text (AF4)
• notice how the writer uses questions in the dialogue (AF5)
• find clues to Roman Britain from the setting of the story (AF7)
Writing
• convert prose to a playscript (AF2)
• write a short section of a playscript using appropriate vocabulary (AF6, AF7)

Questions for guided reading

Starting off

Discuss what the children have learned in history lessons about the Roman invasion of Britain. Remind them where the Romans came from and how Britain differed from Italy (AF7). Ask them to read the play in a group, with different members of the group reading different parts (AF1). As they do so, they should notice how they know when to speak and what to say and do. It will be useful to introduce or remind the children of the meaning of 'layout'.

Read and respond

Use the following questions and prompts as part of a group discussion:
• The Optio talked about mutiny. What does 'mutiny' mean? (AF5)
• **What was the punishment for mutiny? (AF2)**
• **What kind of person is the Optio? (AF3)**
• **What clues did you find to tell you that the play is set in Roman Britain? (AF7)**
• **How does the layout of the text help you to read it? (AF4)**
• **How does the writer tell you where the scene took place? (AF4)**
• How do you know which parts you have to read aloud? (AF4)
• **What have you learned about life for Roman soldiers in Britain? (AF7)**

Going deeper

• **There are six questions in the text. Which ones are not meant to be answered? (AF5)**
• **Why did the Optio ask 'Haven't you remembered anything from your training?' (AF5)**

Reflect

Discuss whether the Optio was a good leader, using quotations from the text to support your ideas. (AF3)

© **Pearson Education Ltd 2010.** APP for Reading and Writing: Year 4

Task 5 The Second Legion by David Orme

Setting: Dorset, England 43 A.D.

Characters:

Manius	a Roman soldier
Titus	a new recruit
Julius	a new recruit
Optio	second in command to a centurion

Scene I: Inside a tent

On the night before their first battle, two young, inexperienced Roman soldiers, Titus and Julius, talk nervously about the day ahead. Manius, an experienced soldier, tells them not to worry. But they are not convinced.

MANIUS: Think, you two! We're the Second Legion! Our commander is the greatest soldier in the Roman army! He looks after his soldiers!

TITUS: If it was down to me, I'd turn around and head back for Rome tomorrow. This is a cold, miserable country!

OPTIO: *(from outside the tent where he has been listening)* You lot! Come out here!

JULIUS: Oh no! It's the Optio!

Task 5 The Second Legion by David Orme

Scene 2: Outside the tent

OPTIO: *(angrily)* Titus and Julius! I might have known! Head back for Rome? That's desertion, Titus. And do you know what the punishment is for mutiny?

TITUS: No, Optio.

OPTIO: Stoning to death!

TITUS: *(frightened)* I didn't mean…

OPTIO: *(in a more kindly tone)* This is your first big battle, isn't it? You need to listen to Manius here. We have got the best commander in the army and the finest centurion in the legion. This Durotriges lot are brave enough, it's true, but what use will their walls and ditches be against our Roman catapults sending fire into their camp?

JULIUS: But how can we get close enough to fight when they are on top of the walls trying to spear us?

OPTIO: Haven't you remembered anything from your training? You use your shield, man! And once we're through the first wall, we all get under our shields and head for the main gate.

MANIUS: Just like a tortoise!

OPTIO: That's right. So I want true Roman bravery from you two tomorrow. And just to make sure, I'll be right behind you – with a very sharp spear!

Task 5 The Second Legion

1. What was the punishment for mutiny?

2. What kind of person is the Optio?

3. What clues did you find to tell you that the play is set in Roman Britain?

4. How does the layout of the text help you to read it?

Task 5 The Second Legion

5. How does the writer tell you where the scene took place?

6. What have you learned about life for
   Roman soldiers in Britain?

7. There are six questions in the text. Which ones are not
   meant to be answered?

8. Why did the Optio ask 'Haven't you remembered
   anything from your training?'

Task 5 The Second Legion

Main Assessment Focus: AF4 (identify and comment on the structure and organisation of texts, including grammatical and presentational features at text level)

Question	Exemplified responses	Grid reference	Notes
How does the layout of the text help you to read it?	Identifies basic features: 'The bits in brackets tell you how to say it.'	Level 3	
	Identifies basic features with comment: 'Your character's name is on the left with his words on the right'; 'There are stage directions to tell you what to do or how to say it.'	Level 4 / bullet 2	
How does the writer tell you where the scene took place?	Identifies basic features of organisation: 'The heading tells you.'	Level 3	
	Identifies basic features with comment: 'After Scene 2 it says "Outside the tent"'; 'There's an introduction that tells you it is in Dorset in England. It tells you what year as well.'	Level 4 / bullet 2	
How do you know which parts you have to read aloud?	Identifies basic features of organisation: 'The characters' names are on the left and their words are next to them.'	Level 3	
	Identifies basic features with comments: 'Your words are to the right of your character's name'; 'It doesn't have words like "said"'; 'You just read the words next to the name.'	Level 4 / bullet 2	

Main Assessment Focus: AF5 (explain and comment on writers' use of language, including grammatical and literary features at word and sentence level)

Question	Exemplified responses	Grid reference	Notes
There are six questions in the text. Which ones are not meant to be answered?	Identifies language features: 'Head back for Rome?'	Level 3	
	Identifies features with comment: '"Head back for Rome?" The Optio knew that they were not really going to do it. It's a good way of showing what he overheard'; '"Haven't you remembered anything from your training?" The Optio said this to remind them of the things they had learned in their training.'	Level 4 / bullet 1	
Why did the Optio ask 'Haven't you remembered anything from your training?'	Identifies language features: 'He was telling them off for forgetting. He just wanted to remind them.'	Level 3	
	Comments on writer's choices: 'He wanted them to remember what to do. He said "Use your shield" because they had learned how to use a shield to stay safe.'	Level 4 / bullet 2	

Main Assessment Focus: AF7 (relate texts to their social, cultural and historical traditions)

Question	Exemplified responses	Grid reference	Notes
What clues did you find to tell you that the play is set in Roman Britain?	Recognises some features: 'It says that Manius was a Roman soldier.'	Level 3 / bullet 2	
	Comments on the historical context: 'It says that it is set in England in 43 A.D. and this is the time when Romans lived in Britain.'	Level 4 / bullet 2	

Exemplified responses matched to levels of attainment are provided as a guide. As always, professional judgement must be used when assessing pupils' learning progression and a range of evidence should be gathered for each AF.

Task 5 The Second Legion

Main Assessment Focus: AF7 cont'd (relate texts to their social, cultural and historical traditions)

Question	Exemplified responses	Grid reference	Notes
What have you learned about life for Roman soldiers in Britain?	Connects text to historical context: 'The punishment for mutiny was stoning to death.'	Level 3 / bullet 1	
	Comments on connection of text and historical context: 'It tells us how soldiers felt about being in Britain. It shows that Roman soldiers weren't happy in Britain and wanted to go back to Rome.'	Level 4 / bullet 1	

Other Assessment Focus: AF2 (understand, describe, select or retrieve information, events or ideas from texts and use quotation and reference to text)

What was the punishment for mutiny?	Identifies basic point from text: 'Killing him.'	Level 3 / bullet 1	
	Comments supported by text reference: 'Stoning to death. If a soldier was in a mutiny they got others to throw stones at him until he died.'	Level 4 / bullet 2	

Other Assessment Focus: AF3 (deduce, infer or interpret information, events or ideas from texts)

What kind of person is the Optio?	Understands meaning at literal level: 'Bad-tempered. He got angry'; 'Kind. He spoke kindly.'	Level 3 / bullet 2	
	Infers meaning: 'A good commander because he helped Titus and Julius to know what to do after telling them off for being scared'; 'He helps them to stop feeling scared.'	Level 4 / bullet 2	

Exemplified responses matched to levels of attainment are provided as a guide. As always, professional judgement must be used when assessing pupils' learning progression and a range of evidence should be gathered for each AF.

Task 5 The Second Legion

1. Here is the next part of *The Second Legion*, but it needs to be written as a playscript. Give it a scene number, setting, list of characters and stage directions.

That night Titus and Julius were in their tent, polishing their shields and swords.

"I don't know if I'm more scared of the Optio or the Durotriges tribe," whispered Julius, holding his sword up in the light of the oil lamp. "When he stares at me, I forget all I learned in training."

"He is kind, even though he's tough. He just wants to be sure we're ready for battle," whispered Titus.

"Yes," said Julius, stretching his aching arms. "A mistake could cost our lives – and others, too."

There was only a snore for an answer.

2. Write the next scene on a separate piece of paper. REMEMBER! Use the rules for writing playscripts.

Task 5 The Second Legion

A pupil response within the range for Level 3 might be:

Question 1 (AF2)

- Characters' names on left; spoken words alongside. Some attempts at stage directions that might include verbs and adverbs. Verbs might not follow playscript style (e.g. 'whispered / he whispered' for 'whispering / whispers'). Most speeches use the exact words from the prose passage.

Question 2 (AF1, AF2, AF6, AF7, AF8)

AF1

There are some appropriate ideas and content: Roman soldiers in their tent near a battlefield; short conversational sentences.

The characters' words are consistent with their roles (the Optio, Manius and the two new recruits).

AF2

Main features of selected form used: scene setting, characters' names to left, followed by colon and no speech marks; stage directions in brackets, including how characters speak – although not in the correct place (positioned after, instead of before, spoken words).

The second legion
Setting: Outside the tent the next morning

OPTIO: COME ON! Titus! Julius! Wake up! its time for battle!

JULIUS: Do we have to? (moaning)

TITUS: Yeay, Optio, do we have to!?

OPTIO: YOU TWO! Stop talking and get on with it!

TITUS AND JULIUS: OK! We'll do it then!

OPTIO: HURRY UP!

MANIUS: Off we go then!

(FIGHT.)

AF6

Uses capital letters, exclamation marks and question marks appropriately throughout the text.

Present tense used in speech.

AF7

Simple, generally appropriate vocabulary – limited range: 'Come on!', 'Hurry up!', 'Off we go then!'

AF8

Common grammatical function words are spelled correctly, although none is difficult.

Contractions are spelled correctly: 'it's', 'we'll'.

There is a phonetically plausible attempt at 'yea' ('yeay').

Task 5 The Second Legion

A pupil response within the range for Level 4 might be:

Question 1 (AF2)
- As for Level 3 but more accurate use of verbs in stage directions:
    Julius (stretching his arms): Yes. A mistake could cost our lives, and others, too.
    Titus (snores): Zzzzzz.

Question 2 (AF1, AF2, AF6, AF7, AF8)

AF1

There are some imaginative ideas, such as the use of colloquial language in the soldiers' speech.

The content is appropriate (Roman soldiers discussing the forthcoming battle).

Ideas are expanded through the use of expanded noun phrases: 'mean fighting machine'.

AF2

Main features of selected form are clear and appropriate to purpose: scene is numbered and given a heading to indicate the setting, characters' names on left, followed by colon and no speech marks; stage directions in brackets, mainly in the appropriate places.

Attempt at humour shows awareness of audience.

Appropriate informal style of speech between soldiers with commanding tone of Optio.

AF6

Accurate demarcation of sentences throughout: capital letters, full stops, exclamation marks, question marks.

Also commas to mark clauses.

AF7

Evidence of deliberate vocabulary choices: 'Barbarians', 'a mean fighting machine'.

AF8

Grammatical function words are spelled correctly, including those with 'ly' endings ('properly', 'quietly') and with multiple morphemes ('therefore', 'possible').

The plural ending of 'yourselves' is spelled incorrectly.

> _The Second Legion_
> Scene4) THE BATTLE
>
> OPTIO: Come on, get yourselfes ready, we've got a battle to win!
>
> TITUS, (quietly): If we don't win then I guess manius will...
>
> MANIUS: You wouldn't be talking about losing now would you Titus? The Roman army is a mean fighting machine. Therefore we just cannot lose!
>
> JULIUS: Well it is possible...
>
> MANIUS: Enough! (Everyone stares at Julius and Manius.)
>
> OPTIO : Out – and fight! (Loud)
>
> MANIUS : Hang on a sec Second, isn't that what Barbarians do; I aint followin' ya!
>
> OPTIO: Do it properly then – tally ho!
>
> (Fight!)

Task 5 The Second Legion

Reading

Next steps for developing AF4

Children will benefit from further practice in answering questions about the structure of texts. Questions like the following will help:

- What do you notice about how the text is set out?
- How does this help you to...?
- How does the writer use the layout to make it easier to...?
- What different types of headings can you find?
- Why does the writer use these?

This activity should be part of a range of evidence gathered for AF4. Other evidence for AF4 can come from sources such as:

- discussions of explanation texts, letters and recounts as well as stories and plays;
- discussions of visuals from informative television programmes;
- guided and shared reading of screen layouts of websites.

Task 2 on pages 19 to 28, Task 3 on pages 29 to 38 and Task 6 on pages 62 to 71 provide other opportunities to gather evidence for AF4.

Next steps for developing AF5

Children will benefit from further practice in answering questions about language and grammatical features. Questions like these will help:

- Which word(s) tells you how x said...?
- Can you find any words, phrases or sentences that are repeated? Explain why.
- How does the writer show that x wants to...?

This activity should be part of a range of evidence gathered for AF5 which could also come from sources such as:

- discussions of passages in which a writer shows how different characters respond to a situation;
- children's enactment of a scene from a play or story;
- discussions of these performances.

All tasks in this book provide opportunities to gather evidence for AF5.

Next steps for developing AF7

You could help the children to explore how social, cultural and historical traditions influence narrative texts and playscripts through discussion points such as:

- How can you tell that the text is set in...?
- Which words and phrases are different to ones used today?
- Could the text be set in a different country / region / period in history? What changes would the writer need to make?

This activity should be part of a range of evidence gathered for AF7, which could also come from sources such as:

- reading / listening to a variety of different texts from different media (e.g. print, online, television) and noticing variations in the type of language used;
- reading narrative texts from different times in history.

Task 1 on pages 8 to 18 provides another opportunity to gather evidence for AF7.

Task 5 The Second Legion

Writing

Next steps for developing AF2

You could encourage children to think about the reader and the content of their written work through discussion points and questions such as:

- How is this type of text used?
- How do you set the scene? How do you show what the characters do and say?
- How can you include anything that is going on in the background?

This should be part of a range of writing activities from which evidence is gathered for AF2. Evidence for AF2 can also be gathered from:

- writing other narrative texts for a specific audience;
- writing a playscript for a specific group of people.

Task 3 on pages 29 to 38 and Task 6 on pages 62 to 71 provide other opportunities to gather evidence for AF2.

Next steps for developing AF6

You could develop the children's understanding of syntax, punctuation and sentence structure through the following activities, discussion and questioning:

- Converting a narrative text to a playscript or vice versa.
- Finding ways to change sentences, including punctuation to create different effects: e.g. to build up tension, create excitement or communicate calm.
- Using commas and connective words when adding ideas or information to sentences.

This should be part of a range of writing activities from which evidence is gathered for AF6. Evidence for AF6 can also be gathered from:

- narrative writing that features complex sentences;
- narrative writing that includes phrases and clauses linked by connectives;
- narrative writing that includes the use of exclamations, questions and sentences with commas and dialogue.

Task 1 on pages 8 to 18 and Task 3 on pages 29 to 38 provide other opportunities to gather evidence for AF6.

Next steps for developing AF7

You could develop the children's vocabulary and their appreciation of the effects of words through activities and discussions such as:

- Picking effective words from their writing and talking about their effects.
- Thinking of better words, phrases or sentences than one or two they used.
- Enacting scenes, considering how a person spoke or moved then asking the children for words to express this: quietly / under his breath.

This should be part of a range of writing activities from which evidence is gathered for AF7. Evidence for AF7 can also be gathered from:

- other narrative writing;
- words used in poetry and persuasive texts the children have written;
- brainstorming words connected with feelings and a particular setting.

Task 2 on pages 19 to 28, Task 4 on pages 39 to 49 and Task 6 on pages 62 to 71 provide other opportunities to gather evidence for AF7.

Task 6 Improving the Neighbourhood

Aims of this task
This task is designed to help you to make judgements about children's attainment in Reading AF2, AF5 and AF6 (with opportunities to assess AF1 and AF4 as well) and Writing AF2, AF3 and AF7 (with opportunities to assess AF1 and AF4 as well). The children read and respond to a persuasive letter from a nine-year-old girl to her local council trying to persuade them to spend their grant money on a mobile library. The children write their own persuasive letter using formal language.

Related Renewed Framework unit
Narrative Unit 4: Persuasive texts

Renewed Framework objectives
7.1, 7.2, 7.5, 9.3, 9.5, 10.1

Key concepts
Reading
- identify main points of a persuasive argument (AF2)
- identify the layout features of a letter (AF4)
- comment on the language and how formal language differs from everyday speech (AF5)
- comment on the purpose of the letter and the opinions expressed by the writer (AF6)

Writing
- choose an issue to write about (AF1)
- write a persuasive letter (AF2)
- plan a persuasive letter in paragraphs (AF3)
- consider and list persuasive words and phrases (AF7)

Questions for guided reading

Starting off
Ensure that the children know that local councils run facilities such as libraries and that they know what is meant by 'community' and 'amenity'. They could name some amenities in their locality. Read the letter (AF1) and check that the children have understood it.

Read and respond
Use the following questions as part of a group discussion:
- **Who, according to Jemma, need a mobile library the most? (AF2)**
- **What are the main points of each paragraph? (AF2)**
- **How can you tell that this is a letter? (AF4)**
- **How is this letter different from a letter that Jemma might write to a friend? (AF5)**

Going deeper
- **What is the purpose of Jemma's letter? (AF6)**
- **Which parts show that the letter is persuasive? (AF5)**
- **What do you think is the best argument Jemma gives? (AF6)**
- **How does she try to make the Council take pity on people? (AF6)**

Reflect
Discuss how the local Council might respond to the letter, and why. What might make them decide to provide a mobile library? (AF6)

Task 6 Improving the Neighbourhood

Wexham Town Council has been given a grant to improve local neighbourhoods. They have asked individuals or groups to suggest an amenity to benefit their community.

24, Kingfisher Lane
Kingbury,
WX27 9SW

Dear Sirs,

<u>Suggestion for a New Community Amenity</u>

I am writing to suggest that the Council spend the grant on a mobile library. Our nearest library is in the town, and it is a journey by two buses to get there. There are lots of people, such as mothers at home with children and the elderly, who find it hard to get there as often as they would like.

I love reading books and it would be great to have a library that I could visit on my own every week. It would also be helpful if the library had an Internet connection so we could order books from the city and county libraries too. It could have big print books for people like my Gran, who have got poor eyesight, and audio books for the blind. Perhaps the library might even have CDs or DVDs that people could rent for a small charge.

I think a mobile library would also be a good place for people to meet up, especially since our local Post Office closed last year. I hope the Council will like my suggestion and decide to pay for a mobile library for our community.

Yours faithfully,

Jemma Harris, aged 9 years

Task 6 Improving the Neighbourhood

1. Who, according to Jemma, need a mobile library the most?

....

....

2. What are the main points of each paragraph?

Paragraph 1: ....

....

....

Paragraph 2: ....

....

....

....

Paragraph 3: ....

....

....

....

3. How can you tell that this is a letter?

....

....

....

....

4. How is this letter different from a letter that Jemma might write to a friend?

....

....

Task 6 Improving the Neighbourhood

5. What is the purpose of Jemma's letter?

6. Which parts show that the letter is persuasive?

7. What do you think is the best argument Jemma gives?

8. How does she try to make the Council take pity on people?

Task 6 Improving the Neighbourhood

Main Assessment Focus: AF2 (understand, describe, select or retrieve information, events or ideas from texts and use quotation and reference to texts)

Question	Exemplified responses	Grid reference	Notes
Who, according to Jemma, need a mobile library the most?	Identifies simple points: 'People who can't get to the town, like mothers with young children and the elderly.'	Level 3 / bullet 1	
	Identifies relevant points and notices that more is said about the elderly than any other group: 'Older people, like Jemma's gran, who find it hard to get to town.'	Level 4 / bullet 1	
What are the main points of each paragraph?	Generally notes main points but might copy or paraphrase the first sentence of a paragraph: 'The nearest library is a journey by two bus rides to get there'; 'Jemma loves reading books.'	Level 3 / bullet 2	
	Main points identified and text summarised: 'The nearest library is a long way away'; 'Jemma could go to a mobile library on her own and it would be useful for others, too.'	Level 4 / bullet 2	

Main Assessment Focus: AF5 (explain and comment on writers' use of language, including grammatical and literary features at word and sentence level)

Question	Exemplified responses	Grid reference	Notes
How is this letter different from a letter that Jemma might write to a friend?	Identifies basic features: 'She wouldn't write about a mobile library, wouldn't write "Sirs". She would write "Love from".'	Level 3	
	Notes that it sounds formal (or other word that suggests this) and gives examples, as above, plus vocabulary used ('long words', 'big words' etc.).	Level 4 / bullet 2	
Which parts show that the letter is persuasive?	Identifies basic features: 'It begins "I am writing to suggest".'	Level 3	
	Identifies and comments on choices: '"I am writing to suggest" makes it look like she is being helpful.' Identifies positive language: 'love', 'great', 'helpful', 'hope'.	Level 4 / bullet 2	

Main Assessment Focus: AF6 (identify and comment on writers' purposes and viewpoints, and the overall effect of the text on the reader)

Question	Exemplified responses	Grid reference	Notes
What is the purpose of Jemma's letter?	Comments identify main purpose: 'She wants a mobile library.'	Level 3 / bullet 1	
	Main purpose identified: 'To persuade the council to spend a grant on a mobile library.'	Level 4 / bullet 1	
What do you think is the best argument Jemma gives?	Identifies points: It is a journey by two bus rides to get to the nearest library / She loves reading / Her gran could get big print books.	Level 3 / bullet 1	
	Identifies subtle persuasive points: 'She tells the Council they could help people like the elderly and mothers with young children.' Might note that library could raise money by hiring CDs / DVDs.	Level 4 / bullet 2	

Other Assessment Focus: AF4 (identify and comment on the structure and organisation of texts, including grammatical and presentational features at text level)

Question	Exemplified responses	Grid reference	Notes
How can you tell that this is a letter?	Identifies a few basic features of organisation: address at the top, use of 'Dear', 'Yours faithfully'.	Level 3	
	Identifies main features: address top right (perhaps says it should have a date), 'Dear' and sign-off, perhaps use of first person.	Level 4 / bullet 2	

Task 6 Improving the Neighbourhood

1. Think of an improvement for your neighbourhood. Write two main reasons why your local Council should carry it out. Support each reason with persuasive evidence.

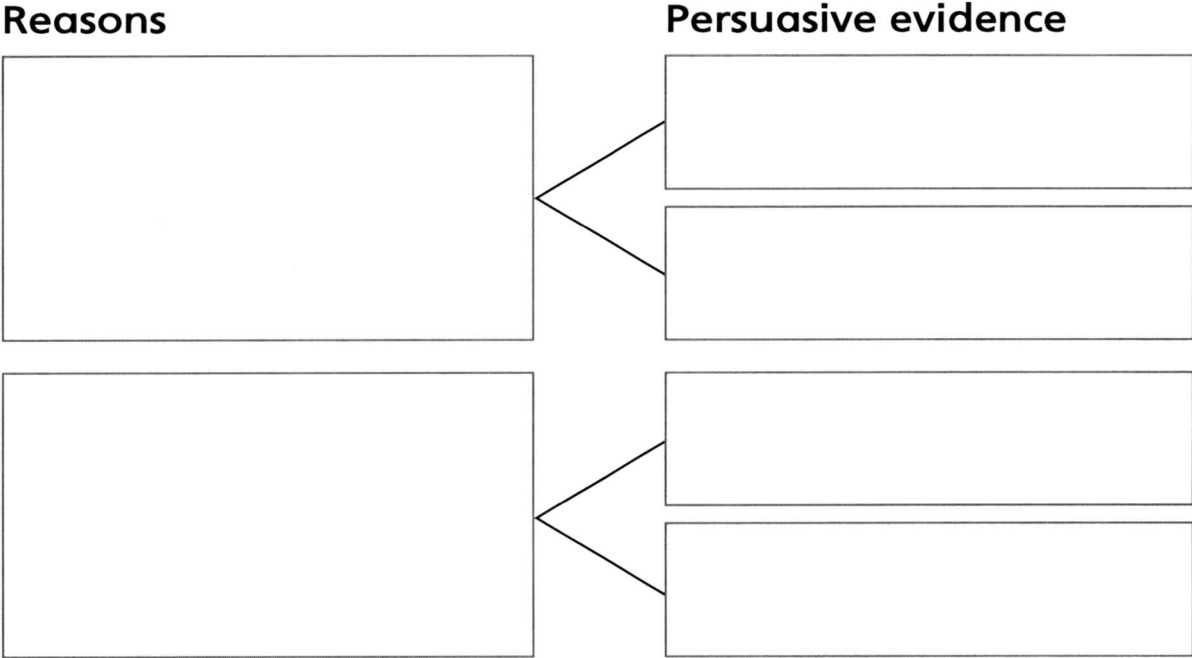

Reasons   Persuasive evidence

2. Think of some persuasive words and phrases you could use in a letter to the Council to persuade them to carry out the improvement.

3. Write your letter on a separate piece of paper.

   REMEMBER!

   • Use the rules for setting out letters.
   • Use paragraphs to organise your ideas.
   • Use powerful and persuasive words and phrases.

Task 6 Improving the Neighbourhood

A pupil response within the range for Level 3 might be:

Question 1 (AF2)

- Lists reasons for the suggested issue and provides some evidence but might not match each piece of evidence to a reason and vice versa.

Question 2 (AF7)

- Vocabulary is simple but appropriate. Uses vocabulary from previous learning: e.g. so, because, so that, surely.

Question 3 (AF1, AF2, AF3, AF4, AF7)

AF1

The content is appropriate and there is an attempt to maintain a viewpoint (that a maze would be a good thing for Chippergardens) with ideas to support this viewpoint.

Elaborates a little on basic information (adverbs – 'I really want', adjectives – 'green', 'brilliant').

AF2

The purpose is established at a general level: he says why he is writing the letter.

There is evidence of awareness of the reader: 'Look forward to hear from you soon'.

The main features of the selected form are signalled: address set out top right, formal opening and signing off. These are mainly in an appropriate style, although he uses 'Yours sincerely' where 'Yours faithfully' would be correct.

AF3

The opening is signalled: 'Dear Sirs or Madams', also the ending: 'Yours sincerely'.

There is some attempt to organise ideas: he introduces the purpose in the first paragraph; in the second paragraph he says that the maze would be a good thing for the village and, in the next paragraph, goes on to explain why. Points in the third paragraph follow a logical sequence.

> 13 Tower Hill
> Chippergardens
> Harts. WD6 9GL
>
> Dear Sirs or Madams,
>
> I am writing to tell you that I really want A MAZE to be built in the village Chippergardens.
>
> I think it would be great for family and friends to meet up.
>
> The maze could be made of bushes and green grass that could be made all around. In the center of the maze there could also be a large picnic/sitting area! This would encourage mums and dads to help thier children so they can relax and enjoy thier day in the middle of the maze. All the children in my class think it would be a brilliant idea so lets hope you do to. We look forward to hear from you soon.
>
> Yours Sincerely

AF4

Some internal structure: two one-sentence paragraphs and then a longer one with ideas loosely organised within, but the final sentence could have been made into a separate summary paragraph.

Pronouns are used as connectives: 'this', 'they'.

AF7

The vocabulary is simple and generally appropriate, mostly with a fairly limited range: 'really', 'great', 'brilliant'.

There are some attempts at selecting words for persuasion: 'encourage', 'relax', 'enjoy', with logical connective ('so').

Task 6 Improving the Neighbourhood

A pupil response within the range for Level 4 might be:

Question 1 (AF2)
- Groups reasons so that they can be linked. Supports reasons with evidence.

Question 2 (AF7)
- As for Level 3, with some more powerful persuasive vocabulary: firstly, lastly, however, certainly, it is clear.

Question 3 (AF1, AF2, AF3, AF4, AF7)

AF1

A viewpoint is established throughout.

The content and ideas are relevant, with some being developed in detail with some use of adverbials ('easily fit a buggy', 'hiding behind flower pots') and expanded noun phrases ('a place where things would be pretty', 'special benches to sit on').

AF2

The main purpose of writing is clear: to persuade the reader that a garden walk-through should be created in the village. She explains the purpose of the letter clearly at the outset.

She uses the main features of letters: address at top right, opening 'Dear Sir or Madam' and signing off with the correct 'Yours faithfully'.

The style is appropriate to the task: fairly formal language for an audience not known to the reader: 'Dear Sir or Madam', 'elderly people', 'it would be suitable', 'raise a committee'. However, the style is not maintained at all times: 'hang out', 'great'.

AF3

Ideas are organised by clustering related points: the first paragraph introduces the idea, the second paragraph says how it would benefit different groups of people, the third paragraph goes on to say how the gardens could be maintained and summarises with the hope that the reader will agree.

AF4

Although paragraphs are used effetively to organise content, cohesion between them is limited to the use of pronouns ('It', 'We'). There is use of simple connectives within paragraphs: 'but', 'and', 'so', 'whilst'.

AF7

There are deliberate vocabulary choices: 'environment', 'suitable', 'elderly people' and expansion of vocabulary to write about the topic ('walk-through', 'raise a committee', 'yours faithfully').

Some expressive words and phrases are used: 'waddle', 'trample', 'go and be'.

> 4 Alexader Road
> Chippergardens
> WDC 48G
>
> Dear Sir or Madam,
>
> I am writing to tell you that I would like a garden walk-through, for the people in Chippergardens. We have lots of woods but no pretty gardens at the common. Chippergardens people, would love a place where things would be pretty and good for the environment.
>
> It would be suitable for all ages and it would be great to have a lovely place where you could go and be. For babies the path through it would be suitable for buggies and pushchairs, so that they could easily fit a buggy or a pushchair and it would go smoothly on the tarmac. Toddlers could waddle around the garden playing with the others. Children could play games like it and stuck in the mud, or they could play hide and seek, hiding behind flower pots and trees. Teenagers could hang out the, but they wouldn't be able to trample on the plants. Adults would have special benches so sit and chat, whilst their children played. Elderly people could sit down too.
>
> We could raise a comitee to water plants and look after everything. I hope you will agree with all my ideas,
>
> Yours faithfully,

Task 6 Improving the Neighbourhood

Reading

Next steps for developing AF2

To develop children's ability to understand, describe, select or retrieve events and ideas from texts, it is useful if they explain any new, technical or difficult words and phrases as well as summarising the main points. Use questions and discussion points such as:

- What does... mean?
- Give as many reasons as you can to support [Jemma's] view that [the village needs a mobile library].

This activity should be part of a range of evidence gathered for AF2. Evidence for AF2 could come from various sources, such as:

- reading printed advertisements: e.g. in magazines, newspapers, comics;
- listening to radio advertisements and watching them on television;
- browsing appropriate internet advertisements;
- identifying how advertisements appeal to their audience;
- making notes on the main points of arguments related to issues in history or citizenship topics.

All tasks in this book provide opportunities to gather evidence for AF2.

Next steps for developing AF5

Children will benefit from further practice in answering questions about language and grammatical features and identifying these in texts. Questions and discussion points like those below will be helpful when reading a piece of text together:

- Which words and phrases are examples of persuasive language?
- Which words and phrases show that the language is formal?

This activity should be part of a range of evidence gathered for AF5 which could also come from sources, such as:

- discussions of the language of formal and informal persuasive texts, such as newspaper articles, leaflets, advertisements and transcribed dialogue;
- comparing formal letters and letters to family and friends;
- responses to formal and informal radio and television broadcasts;
- comparing the language of emails, text messages and letters.

All tasks in this book provide opportunities to gather evidence for AF5.

Next steps for developing AF6

You could develop the children's understanding of writers' viewpoints and purposes through questions such as:

- Why did x write this? How can you tell?
- Who is meant to read it?
- How does the writer want readers to feel when they read this?

This activity should be part of a range of evidence gathered for AF6 which could also come from sources such as:

- reading a variety of different persuasive texts from different media (e.g. print, online, television) and identifying their purpose;
- evaluating the effectiveness of persuasive texts such as advertisements and film trailers;
- writing letters to the Council or newspapers;
- discussing the purposes of letters in newspapers, magazines and comics.

Task 2 on pages 19 to 28, Task 3 on pages 29 to 38 and Task 4 on pages 39 to 49 provide other opportunities to gather evidence for AF6.

Task 6 Improving the Neighbourhood

Writing

Next steps for developing AF2

You could help children to think about the intended reader of a persuasive letter through discussion points and questions such as:

- Who is going to read what you write?
- What kind of information will help you to persuade them?
- Why might the reader disagree with you: e.g. the cost might be too high, they might have other plans? Include some arguments against these.

This should be part of a range of writing activities from which evidence is gathered for AF2. Evidence for AF2 can also be gathered from:

- writing other non-fiction texts for a specific audience: e.g. news recounts for people interested in a specific topic (e.g. sport, fashion);
- writing narrative texts for specific age groups.

Task 3 on pages 29 to 38 and Task 5 on pages 50 to 61 provide other opportunities to gather evidence for AF2.

Next steps for developing AF3

You could develop the children's understanding of how to organise and present persuasive letters through discussion points and activities such as:

- Using mind maps for recording the main points to include, then using lines to link ideas that are related to one another and then grouping them in paragraphs.
- Writing a sentence to open the letter and another to end it. Sharing these ideas with a partner and discussing whether they can be improved and, if so, how.
- Asking them to read a partner's letter and think up an argument against a point in the letter. Responding to the challenge.

This should be part of a range of writing activities from which evidence is gathered for AF3. Evidence for AF3 can also be gathered from:

- planning, organising and writing other types of persuasive text;
- planning, organising and writing other non-fiction texts;
- planning and writing narrative texts and poetry that express a point of view.

Task 1 on pages 8 to 18, Task 3 on pages 29 to 38 and Task 4 on pages 39 to 49 provide other opportunities to gather evidence for AF3.

Next steps for developing AF7

You could develop the children's topic vocabulary and the range of persuasive language they use through activities and discussions such as:

- Picking out effective words and phrases from their writing and talking about their effects: e.g. 'it would be suitable', 'people would...', 'there could'.
- Improving words, phrases or sentences: e.g. replacing 'good' or 'great' with the reasons why it would be (e.g. 'It would provide enjoyment and improve the area').
- Improving connectives and persuasive words and phrases: e.g. 'so', 'because', 'now that', 'according to', 'if', 'surely', 'it is clear', 'clearly', 'finally'.

This should be part of a range of writing activities from which evidence is gathered for AF7. Evidence for AF7 can also be gathered from:

- word lists connected with topics the children have studied in other subjects;
- previous work on the connotations of words;
- brainstorming words connected with persuasion.

Task 2 on pages 19 to 28, Task 4 on pages 39 to 49 and Task 5 on pages 50 to 61 provide other opportunities to gather evidence for AF7.

Acknowledgements

The publisher would like to thank St. Paul's C of E Primary School, Chipperfield for its invaluable help with producing children's writing samples for this book.

The publisher would like to thank the following for permission to use their copyright material.

Text

Reading and Writing Assessment Guidelines (on pages 6–7) © Crown copyright 2009, reproduced under the terms of the Click-Use Licence.

Extract from *Tom's Private War* by Robert Leeson (Puffin, 1998). Copyright © Robert Leeson, 1998. Used by permisssion of Penguin Books UK Limited.

Extract from *Until I met Dudley: How everyday things really work* by Douglas Maxwell and Roger McGough. Published by Frances Lincoln Ltd. Copyright © 1999. Reproduced by permission of Frances Lincoln Ltd.

Every effort has been made to contact copyright holders of material reproduced in this book. Any omissions will be rectified in subsequent printings if notice is given to the publishers.